ESSAYS OF ROBERT LOUIS STEVENSON

SELECTED AND EDITED WITH AN INTRODUCTION AND NOTES BY

WILLIAM LYON PHELPS

British Library Cataloguing-in-Publication Data
A catalogue record for this book is available from the
British Library

Contents

William Lyon Phelps

William Lyon Phelps was born on 2nd January 1865, in New Haven, Conneticut, United States.

Phelps earned a B.A. in 1887, writing his thesis on the Idealism of George Berkeley. He then gained an M.A. in 1891 from Yale and his PhD from Harvard in the same year. During his time a Yale, he offered a course in modern novels which brought the university considerable attention both nationally and internationally. This was quite controversial at the time and Phelps was pressured to give up the course, but eventually, due to popular demand, reinstated it outside the official curriculum.

In 1892, Phelps married Annabel Hubbard, sister of childhood friend Frank Hubbard, and the couple moved to the family estate overlooking Lake Huron. Phelps christened it "The House of the Seven Gables", after the Nathanial Hawthorne story of the same name.

He became a very popular figure at Yale but also as an inspirational orator. He went on lecture tours that drew large audiences, speaking on the virtues of modern literature. He also preached regularly at the Huron City Methodist Episcopal Church and attracted such large crowds that the church was remodelled twice in five years to accommodate them.

Phelps published many essays on modern and European literature, including titles such as *Essays on Modern Novelists* (1910), *Some Makers of American Literature* (1923), and *As I Like it* (1923).

After his retirement from Yale in 1933, after 41 years of service, Phelps continued his public speaking, preaching, and writing a newspaper column. He also sat on book selection committees and acted as a judge for the Pulitzer Prize for literature.

His wife, Annabel, died from a stroke in 1939 and Phelps died four years later, in 1943.

PREFACE

The text of the following essays is taken from the Thistle Edition of Stevenson's *Works*, published by Charles Scribner's Sons, in New York. I have refrained from selecting any of Stevenson's formal essays in literary criticism, and have chosen only those that, while ranking among his masterpieces in style, reveal his personality, character, opinions, philosophy, and faith. In the *Introduction*, I have endeavoured to be as brief as possible, merely giving a sketch of his life, and indicating some of the more notable sides of his literary achievement; pointing out also the literary school to which these Essays belong. A lengthy critical Introduction to a book of this kind would be an impertinence to the general reader, and a nuisance to a teacher. In the *Notes*, I have aimed at simple explanation and some extended literary comment. It is hoped that the general recognition of Stevenson as an English classic may make this volume useful in school and college courses, while it is not too much like a textbook to repel the average reader. I am indebted to Professor Catterall of Cornell and to Professor Cross of Yale, and to my brother the Rev. Dryden W. Phelps, for some assistance in locating references. W.L.P., YALE UNIVERSITY, *13 February 1906.*

INTRODUCTION

I

LIFE OF STEVENSON

Robert Louis Stevenson[1] was born at Edinburgh on the 13 November 1850. His father, Thomas, and his grandfather, Robert, were both distinguished light-house engineers; and the maternal grandfather, Balfour, was a Professor of Moral Philosophy, who lived to be ninety years old. There was, therefore, a combination of *Lux et Veritas* in the blood of young Louis Stevenson, which in *Dr. Jekyll and Mr. Hyde* took the form of a luminous portrayal of a great moral idea.

In the language of Pope, Stevenson's life was a long disease. Even as a child, his weak lungs caused great anxiety to all the family except himself; but although Death loves a shining mark, it took over forty years of continuous practice for the grim archer to send the black arrow home. It is perhaps fortunate for English literature that his health was no better; for the boy craved an active life, and would doubtless have become an engineer. He made a brave attempt to pursue this calling, but it was soon evident that his constitution made it impossible. After desultory schooling, and an immense amount of general reading, he entered the University of Edinburgh, and then tried the study of law. Although the thought of this profession became more and more repugnant, and finally intolerable, he passed his final examinations satisfactorily. This was in 1875.

He had already begun a series of excursions to the south of France and other places, in search of a climate more favorable to his incipient malady; and every return to Edinburgh proved more and more conclusively that he could not live in Scotch mists. He had made the acquaintance of a number of literary men, and he was consumed with a burning ambition to become a writer. Like Ibsen's *Master-Builder*, there was a troll in his blood, which drew him away to the continent on inland voyages with a canoe and lonely tramps with a donkey; these gave him material for books full of brilliant pictures, shrewd observations, and irrepressible humour. He contributed various articles to magazines, which were immediately recognised by critics like Leslie Stephen as bearing the unmistakable mark of literary genius; but they attracted almost no attention from the general reading public, and their author had only the consciousness of good work for his reward. In 1880 he was married.

Stevenson's first successful work was *Treasure Island*, which was published in book form in 1883, and has already become a classic. This did not, however, bring him either a good income or general fame. His great reputation dates from the publication of the *Strange Case of Dr. Jekyll and Mr. Hyde,* which appeared in 1886. That work had an instant and unqualified success, especially in America, and made its author's name known to the whole English-speaking world. *Kidnapped* was published the same year, and another masterpiece, *The Master of Ballantrae,* in 1889.

After various experiments with different climates, including that of Switzerland, Stevenson sailed for America in August 1887. The winter of 1887-88 he spent at Saranac Lake, under the care of Dr. Trudeau, who became one of his best friends. In 1890 he settled at Samoa in the Pacific. Here he entered upon a career of intense literary activity, and yet found time to take an active part in the politics of the island, and to give valuable assistance in internal improvements.

The end came suddenly, exactly as he would have wished it, and precisely as he had unconsciously predicted in the last radiant, triumphant sentences of his great essay, *Aes Triplex.* He had been at work on a novel, *St. Ives,* one of his poorer efforts, and whose composition grew steadily more and more distasteful, until he found that he was actually writing against the grain. He threw this aside impatiently, and with extraordinary energy and enthusiasm began a new story, *Weir of Hermiston,* which would undoubtedly have been his masterpiece, had he lived to complete it. In luminosity of style, in nobleness of conception, in the almost infallible choice of words, this astonishing fragment easily takes first place in Stevenson's productions. At the end of a day spent in almost feverish dictation, the third of December 1894, he suddenly fainted, and died without regaining consciousness. "Death had not been suffered to take so much as an illusion from his heart. In the hot-fit of life, a-tiptoe on the highest point of being, he passed at a bound on to the other side. The noise of the mallet and chisel was scarcely quenched, the trumpets were hardly done blowing, when, trailing with him clouds of glory, this happy-starred, full-blooded spirit shot into the spiritual land."

He was buried at the summit of a mountain, the body being carried on the shoulders of faithful Samoans, who might have sung Browning's noble hymn,

> "Let us begin and carry up this corpse,
>   Singing together!
> Leave we the common crofts, the vulgar thorpes
>   Each in its tether
> Sleeping safe on the bosom of the plain…
> That's the appropriate country; there, man's thought,
>   Rarer, intenser,
> Self-gathered for an outbreak, as it ought,
>   Chafes in the censer.
> Leave we the unlettered plain its herd and crop;

Seek we sepulture
On a tall mountain…
Thither our path lies; wind we up the heights:
  Wait ye the warning!
Our low life was the level's and the night's;
  He's for the morning.
Step to a tune, square chests, erect each head,
  'Ware the beholders!
This is our master, famous, calm and dead,
  Borne on our shoulders…

Here—here's his place, where meteors shoot clouds
form,
      Lightnings are loosened,
Stars come and go! Let joy break with the storm,
      Peace let the dew send!
Lofty designs must close in like effects
      Loftily lying,
Leave him—still loftier than the world suspects,
      Living and dying."

II

PERSONALITY AND CHARACTER

Stevenson had a motley personality, which is sufficiently evident in his portraits. There was in him the Puritan, the man of the world, and the vagabond. There was something too of the obsolete soldier of fortune, with the cocked and feathered hat, worn audaciously on one side. There was also a touch of the elfin, the uncanny—the mysterious charm that belongs to the borderland between the real and the unreal world—the element so conspicuous and so indefinable in the art of Hawthorne. Writers so different as Defoe, Cooper, Poe, and Sir Thomas Browne, are seen with varying degrees of emphasis in his literary temperament. He was whimsical as an imaginative child; and everyone has noticed that he never grew old. His buoyant optimism was based on a chronic experience of physical pain, for pessimists like Schopenhauer are usually men in comfortable circumstances, and of excellent bodily health. His courage and cheerfulness under depressing circumstances are so splendid to contemplate that some critics believe that in time his *Letters* may be regarded as his greatest literary work, for they are priceless in their unconscious revelation of a beautiful soul.

Great as Stevenson was as a writer, he was still greater as a Man. So many admirable books have been written by men whose character will not bear examination, that it is refreshing to find one Master-Artist whose daily life was so full of the fruits of the spirit. As his romances have brought pleasure to thousands of readers, so the spectacle of his cheerful march through the Valley of the Shadow of Death is a constant source of comfort and inspiration. One feels ashamed of cowardice and petty irritation after witnessing the steady courage of this man. His philosophy of life is totally different from that of Stoicism; for the Stoic says, "Grin and bear it," and usually succeeds in doing neither. Stevenson seems to say, "Laugh and forget it," and he showed us how to do both.

Stevenson had the rather unusual combination of the Artist and the
Moralist, both elements being marked in his writings to a very high
degree. The famous and oft-quoted sonnet by his friend, the late Mr.
Henley, gives a vivid picture:

"Thin-legged, thin-chested, slight unspeakably,
Neat-footed and weak-fingered: in his face—
Lean, large-honed, curved of beak, and touched with

race,

Bold-lipped, rich-tinted, mutable as the sea,
The brown eyes radiant with vivacity—
There shown a brilliant and romantic grace,
A spirit intense and rare, with trace on trace
Of passion, impudence, and energy.
Valiant in velvet, light in ragged luck,
Most vain, most generous, sternly critical,
Buffoon and poet, lover and sensualist;
A deal of Ariel, just a streak of Puck,
Much Antony, of Hamlet most of all,
And something of the Shorter Catechist."

He was not primarily a moral teacher, like Socrates or Thomas Carlyle; nor did he feel within him the voice of a prophetic mission. The virtue of his writings consists in their wholesome ethical quality, in their solid health. Fresh air is often better for the soul than the swinging of the priest's censer. At a time when the school of Zola was at its climax, Stevenson opened the windows and let in the pleasant breeze. For the morbid and unhealthy period of adolescence, his books are more healthful than many serious moral works. He purges the mind of uncleanness, just as he purged contemporary fiction.

As Stevenson's correspondence with his friends like Sidney Colvin and William Archer reveals the social side of his nature, so his correspondence with the Unseen Power in which he believed shows that his character was essentially religious. A man's letters are often a truer picture of his mind than a photograph; and when these epistles are directed not to men and women, but to the Supreme Intelligence, they form a real revelation of their writer's heart. Nothing betrays the personality of a man more clearly than his prayers, and the following petition that Stevenson composed for the use of his household at Vailima, bears the stamp of its author.

"At Morning. The day returns and brings us the petty round of irritating concerns and duties. Help us to play the man, help us to perform them with laughter and kind faces, let cheerfulness abound with industry. Give us to go blithely on our business all this day, bring us to our resting beds weary and content and undishonoured, and grant us in the end the gift of sleep."

III

STEVENSON'S VERSATILITY

Stevenson was a poet, a dramatist, an essayist, and a novelist, besides writing many political, geographical, and biographical sketches. As a poet, his fame is steadily waning.

The tendency at first was to rank him too high, owing to the undeniable charm of many of the poems in the *Child's Garden of Verses*. The child's view of the world, as set forth in these songs, is often originally and gracefully expressed; but there is little in Stevenson's poetry that is of permanent value, and it is probable that most of it will be forgotten. This fact is in a way a tribute to his genius; for his greatness as a prose writer has simply eclipsed his reputation as a poet.

His plays were failures. They illustrate the familiar truth that a man may have positive genius as a dramatic writer, and yet fail as a dramatist. There are laws that govern the stage which must be obeyed; play-writing is a great art in itself, entirely distinct from literary composition. Even Browning, the most intensely dramatic poet of the nineteenth century, was not nearly so successful in his dramas as in his dramatic lyrics and romances.

His essays attracted at first very little attention; they were too fine and too subtle to awaken popular enthusiasm. It was the success of his novels that drew readers back to the essays, just as it was the vogue of Sudermann's plays that made his earlier novels popular. One has only to read such essays, however, as those printed in this volume to realise not only their spirit and charm, but to feel instinctively that one is reading English Literature. They are exquisite works of art, written in an almost impeccable style. By many judicious readers, they are placed above his works of fiction. They certainly constitute the most original portion of his entire literary output. It is astonishing that this young Scotchman should have been able to make so many actually new observations on a game so old as Life. There is a shrewd insight into the motives of human conduct that makes some of these graceful sketches belong to the literature of philosophy, using the word philosophy in its deepest and broadest sense. The essays are filled with whimsical paradoxes, keen and witty as those of Bernard Shaw, without having any of the latter's cynicism, iconoclasm, and sinister attitude toward morality. For the real foundation of even the lightest of Stevenson's works is invariably ethical.

His fame as a writer of prose romances grows brighter every year. His supreme achievement was to show that a book might be crammed with the most wildly exciting incidents, and yet reveal profound and acute analysis of character, and be written with consummate art. His tales have all the fertility of invention and breathless suspense of Scott and Cooper, while in literary style they immeasurably surpass the finest work of these two great masters.

His best complete story, is, I think, *Treasure Island*. There is a peculiar brightness about this book which even the most notable of the later works failed to equal. Nor was it a trifling feat to make a blind man and a one-legged man so formidable that even the reader is afraid of them. Those who complain that this is merely a pirate story forget that in art the subject is of comparatively little importance, whereas the treatment is everything. To say, as some do, that there is no difference between *Treasure Island* and a cheap tale of blood and thunder, is equivalent to saying that there is no difference between the Sistine Madonna and a chromo Virgin.

IV

THE PERSONAL ESSAY

The Personal Essay is a peculiar form of literature, entirely different from critical essays like those of Matthew Arnold and from purely reflective essays, like those of Bacon. It is a species of writing somewhat akin to autobiography or firelight conversation; where the writer takes the reader entirely into his confidence, and chats pleasantly with him on topics that may be as widely apart as the immortality of the soul and the proper colour of a necktie. The first and supreme master of this manner of writing was Montaigne, who belongs in the front rank of the world's greatest writers of prose. Montaigne talks endlessly on the most trivial subjects without ever becoming trivial. To those who really love reading and have some sympathy with humanity,

Montaigne's *Essays* are a "perpetual refuge and delight," and it is interesting to reflect how far in literary fame this man, who talked about his meals, his horse, and his cat, outshines thousands of scholarly and talented writers, who discussed only the most serious themes in politics and religion. The great English prose writers in the field of the personal essay during the seventeenth century were Sir Thomas Browne, Thomas Fuller, and Abraham Cowley, though Walton's *Compleat Angler* is a kindred work. Browne's *Religio Medici*, and his delightful *Garden of Cyrus*, old Tom Fuller's quaint *Good Thoughts in Bad Times* and Cowley's charming *Essays* are admirable examples of this school of composition. Burton's wonderful *Anatomy of Melancholy* is a colossal personal essay. Some of the papers of Steele and Addison in the *Tatler*, *Guardian,* and the *Spectator* are of course notable; but it was not until the appearance of Charles Lamb that the personal essay reached its climax in English literature. Over the pages of the *Essays of Elia* hovers an immortal charm—the charm of a nature inexhaustible in its humour and kindly sympathy for humanity. Thackeray was another great master of the literary easy-chair, and is to some readers more attractive in this attitude than as a novelist. In America we have had a few writers who have reached eminence in this form, beginning with Washington Irving, and including Donald G. Mitchell, whose *Reveries of a Bachelor* has been read by thousands of people for over fifty years.

As a personal essayist Stevenson seems already to belong to the first rank. He is both eclectic and individual. He brought to his pen the reminiscences of varied reading, and a wholly original touch of fantasy. He was literally steeped in the gorgeous Gothic diction of the seventeenth century, but he realised that such a prose style as illumines the pages of William Drummond's *Cypress Grove* and Browne's *Urn Burial* was a lost art. He attempted to imitate such writing only in his youthful exercises, for his own genius was forced to express itself in an original way. All of his personal essays have that air of distinction which attracts and holds one's attention as powerfully in a book as it does in social intercourse. Everything that he has to say seems immediately worth saying, and worth hearing, for he was one of those rare men who had an interesting mind. There are some literary artists who have style and nothing else, just as there are some great singers who have nothing but a voice. The true test of a book, like that of an individual, is whether or not it improves upon acquaintance. Stevenson's essays reflect a personality that becomes brighter as we draw nearer. This fact makes his essays not merely entertaining reading, but worthy of serious and prolonged study.

[Note 1: His name was originally Robert Lewis Balfour Stevenson. He later dropped the "Balfour" and changed the spelling of "Lewis" to "Louis," but the name was always pronounced "Lewis."]

BIBLIOGRAPHY

The following information is taken from Col. Prideaux's admirable *Bibliography* of Stevenson, London, 1903. I have given the titles and dates of only the more important publications in book form; and of the critical works on Stevenson, I have included only a few of those that seem especially useful to the student and general reader. The detailed facts about the separate publications of each essay included in the present volume are fully given in my notes.

WORKS

1878. An Inland Voyage. 1879. Travels with a Donkey. 1881. Virginibus Puerisque. 1882. Familiar Studies of Men and Books. 1882. New Arabian Nights. 1883. Treasure Island. 1885. Prince Otto. 1885. A Child's Garden of Verses. 1885. More New Arabian Nights. The Dynamiter. 1886. Strange Case of Dr. Jekyll and Mr. Hyde. 1886. Kidnapped. 1887. The Merry Men. 1887. Memories and Portraits. 1888. The Black Arrow. 1889. The Master of Ballantrae. (A few copies privately printed in 1888.) 1889. The Wrong Box. 1890. Father Damien. 1892. Across the Plains. 1892. The Wrecker. 1893. Island Nights' Entertainments. 1893. Catriona. 1894. The Ebb Tide. 1895. Vailima Letters. 1896. Weir of Hermiston. 1898. St. Ives. 1899. Letters, Two Volumes.

NOTE. The *Edinburgh Edition* of the *works*, in twenty-eight volumes, is often referred to by bibliographers; it can now be obtained only at second-hand bookshops, or at auction sales. The best complete edition on the market is the *Thistle Edition*, in twenty-six volumes, including the *Life* and the *Letters*, published by Charles Scribner's Sons, New York.

WORKS ON STEVENSON

Life of Robert Louis Stevenson, by Graham Balfour. 1901. Two Volumes. *This is the standard Life, and indispensable.*

Robert Louis Stevenson, by Henry James, in *Partial Portraits*, 1894. *Admirable criticism.*

Robert Louis Stevenson, by Walter Raleigh. 1895. *An excellent appreciation of his character and work.*

Robert Louis Stevenson: Personal Memories, by Edmund Gosse, in *Critical Kit-Kats*, 1896. *Entertaining gossip.*

Stevenson's Shrine, The Record of a Pilgrimage, by Laura Stubbs. 1903. *Very interesting full-page illustrations.*

(For further critical books and articles, which are numerous, consult Prideaux.)

ESSAYS OF ROBERT LOUIS
STEVENSON

I

ON THE ENJOYMENT OF UNPLEASANT PLACES

It is a difficult matter[1] to make the most of any given place, and we have much in our own power. Things looked at patiently from one side after another generally end by showing a side that is beautiful. A few months ago some words were said in the *Portfolio* as to an "austere regimen in scenery"; and such a discipline was then recommended as "healthful and strengthening to the taste." That is the text, so to speak, of the present essay. This discipline in scenery,[2] it must be understood, is something more than a mere walk before breakfast to whet the appetite. For when we are put down in some unsightly neighborhood, and especially if we have come to be more or less dependent on what we see, we must set ourselves to hunt out beautiful things with all the ardour and patience of a botanist after a rare plant. Day by day we perfect ourselves in the art of seeing nature more favourably. We learn to live with her, as people learn to live with fretful or violent spouses: to dwell lovingly on what is good, and shut our eyes against all that is bleak or inharmonious. We learn, also, to come to each place in the right spirit. The traveller, as Brantôme quaintly tells us, "*fait des discours en soi pour se soutenir en chemin*";[3] and into these discourses he weaves something out of all that he sees and suffers by the way; they take their tone greatly from the varying character of the scene; a sharp ascent brings different thoughts from a level road; and the man's fancies grow lighter as he comes out of the wood into a clearing. Nor does the scenery any more affect the thoughts than the thoughts affect the scenery. We see places through our humours as though differently colored glasses. We are ourselves a term in the equation, a note of the chord, and make discord or harmony almost at will. There is no fear for the result, if we can but surrender ourselves sufficiently to the country that surrounds and follows us, so that we are ever thinking suitable thoughts or telling ourselves some suitable sort of story as we go. We become thus, in some sense, a centre of beauty; we are provocative of beauty,[4] much as a gentle and sincere character is provocative of sincerity and gentleness in others. And even where there is no harmony to be elicited by the quickest and most obedient of spirits, we may still embellish a place with some attraction of romance. We may learn to go far afield for associations, and handle them lightly when we have found them. Sometimes an old print comes to our aid; I have seen many a spot lit up at once with picturesque imaginations, by a reminiscence of Callot, or Sadeler, or Paul Brill.[5] Dick Turpin[6] has been my lay figure for many an English lane. And I suppose the Trossachs would hardly be the Trossachs[7] for most tourists if a man of admirable romantic instinct had not peopled it for them with harmonious figures, and brought them thither their minds rightly prepared for the impression. There is half the battle in this preparation. For instance: I have rarely been able to visit, in the proper spirit, the wild and inhospitable places of our own Highlands. I am happier where it is tame and fertile, and not readily pleased without trees.[8] I understand that there are some phases of mental trouble that harmonise well with such surroundings, and that some persons, by the dispensing power of the imagination, can go back several centuries in spirit, and put themselves into sympathy with the hunted, houseless, unsociable way of life that was in its place upon these savage hills. Now, when I am sad, I like nature to charm me out of my sadness, like David before Saul;[9] and the thought of these past ages strikes nothing in me but an unpleasant pity; so that I can never hit on the right humour for this sort of landscape, and lose much pleasure in consequence. Still, even here, if I were only let alone, and time enough were given, I should have all manner of pleasure, and take many clear and beautiful images away with me when I left. When we cannot think ourselves into sympathy with the great features of a country, we learn to ignore them, and put our head among the grass for flowers, or pore, for long times together, over the changeful current of a stream. We come down to the sermon in stones,[10] when we are shut out from any poem in the spread landscape. We begin to peep and botanise, we take an interest in birds and insects, we find many things beautiful in miniature. The reader will recollect the little summer scene in *Wuthering Heights*[11]—the one warm scene, perhaps, in all that powerful, miserable novel—and the great feature that is made therein by grasses and flowers and a little sunshine: this is in the spirit of which I now speak. And, lastly, we can go indoors; interiors are sometimes as beautiful, often more picturesque, than the shows of the open air, and they have that quality of shelter of which I shall presently have more to say.

With all this in mind, I have often been tempted to put forth the paradox that any place is good enough to live a life in, while it is only in a few, and those highly favoured, that we can pass a few hours agreeably. For, if we only stay long enough, we become at home in the neighbourhood. Reminiscences spring up, like flowers, about uninteresting corners. We forget to some degree the superior loveliness of other places, and fall into a tolerant and sympathetic spirit which is its own reward and justification. Looking back the other day on some recollections of my own, I was astonished to find how much I owed to such a residence; six weeks in one unpleasant country-side had done more, it seemed, to quicken and educate my sensibilities than many years in places that jumped more nearly with my inclination.

The country to which I refer was a level and treeless plateau, over which the winds cut like a whip. For miles on miles it was the same. A river, indeed, fell into the sea near the town where I resided; but the valley of the river was shallow and bald, for as far up as ever I had the heart to follow it. There were roads, certainly, but roads that had no beauty or interest; for, as there was no timber, and but little irregularity of surface, you saw your whole walk exposed to you from the beginning: there was nothing left to fancy, nothing to expect, nothing to see by the wayside, save here and there an unhomely-looking homestead, and here and there a solitary, spectacled stone-breaker;[12] and you were only accompanied, as you went doggedly forward by the gaunt telegraph-posts and the hum of the resonant wires in the keen sea-wind. To one who has learned to know their song in warm pleasant places by the Mediterranean, it seemed to taunt the country, and make it still bleaker by suggested contrast. Even the waste places by the side of the road were not, as Hawthorne liked to put it, "taken back to Nature" by any decent covering of vegetation. Wherever the land had the chance, it seemed to lie fallow. There is a certain tawny nudity of the South, bare sunburnt plains, coloured like a lion, and hills clothed only in the blue transparent air; but this was of another description—this was the nakedness of the North; the earth seemed to know that it was naked, and was ashamed and cold.[13]

It seemed to be always blowing on that coast. Indeed, this had passed into the speech of the inhabitants, and they saluted each other when they met with "Breezy, breezy," instead of the customary "Fine day" of farther south. These continual winds were not like the harvest breeze, that just keeps an equable pressure against your face as you walk, and serves to set all the trees talking over your head, or bring round you the smell of the wet surface of the country after a shower. They were of the bitter, hard, persistent sort, that interferes with sight and respiration, and makes the eyes sore. Even such winds as these have their own merit in proper time and place. It is pleasant to see them brandish great masses of shadow. And what a power they have over the colour of the world! How they ruffle the solid woodlands in their passage, and make them shudder and whiten like a single willow! There is nothing more vertiginous than a wind like this among the woods, with all its sights and noises; and the effect gets between some painters and their sober eyesight, so that, even when the rest of their picture is calm, the foliage is coloured like foliage in a gale.[14] There was nothing, however, of this sort to be noticed in a country where there were no trees and hardly any shadows, save the passive shadows and clouds or those of rigid houses and walls. But the wind was nevertheless an occasion of pleasure; for nowhere could you taste more fully the pleasure of a sudden lull, or a place of opportune shelter. The reader knows what

I mean; he must remember how, when he has sat himself down behind a dyke on a hill-side, he delighted to hear the wind hiss vainly through the crannies at his back; how his body tingled all over with warmth, and it began to dawn upon him, with a sort of slow surprise, that the country was beautiful, the heather purple, and the faraway hills all marbled with sun and shadow. Wordsworth, in a beautiful passage[15] of the "Prelude," has used this as a figure for the feeling struck in us by the quiet by-streets of London after the uproar of the great thoroughfares; and the comparison may be turned the other way with as good effect:

"Meanwhile the roar continues, till at length,
Escaped as from an enemy we turn,
Abruptly into some sequestered nook,
Still as a shelter'd place when winds blow loud!"

I remember meeting a man once, in a train, who told me of what must have been quite the most perfect instance of this pleasure of escape. He had gone up, one sunny, windy morning, to the top of a great cathedral somewhere abroad; I think it was Cologne Cathedral, the great unfinished marvel by the Rhine;[16] and after a long while in dark stairways, he issued at last into the sunshine, on a platform high above the town. At that elevation it was quite still and warm; the gale was only in the lower strata of the air, and he had forgotten it in the quiet interior of the church and during his long ascent; and so you may judge of his surprise when, resting his arms on the sunlit balustrade and looking over into the *Place* far below him, he saw the good people holding on their hats and leaning hard against the wind as they walked. There is something, to my fancy, quite perfect in this little experience of my fellow-traveller's. The ways of men seem always very trivial to us when we find ourselves alone on a church-top, with the blue sky and a few tall pinnacles, and see far below us the steep roofs and foreshortened buttresses, and the silent activity of the city streets; but how much more must they not have seemed so to him as he stood, not only above other men's business, but above other men's climate, in a golden zone like Apollo's![17]

This was the sort of pleasure I found in the country of which I write. The pleasure was to be out of the wind, and to keep it in memory all the time, and hug oneself upon the shelter. And it was only by the sea that any such sheltered places were to be found. Between the black worm-eaten headlands there are little bights and havens, well screened from the wind and the commotion of the external sea, where the sand and weeds look up into the gazer's face from a depth of tranquil water, and the sea-birds, screaming and flickering from the ruined crags, alone disturb the silence and the sunshine. One such place has impressed itself on my memory beyond all others. On a rock by the water's edge, old fighting men of the Norse breed had planted a double castle; the two stood wall to wall like semi-detached villas; and yet feud had run so high between their owners, that one, from out of a window, shot the other as he stood in his own doorway. There is something in the juxtaposition of these two enemies full of tragic irony. It is grim to think of bearded men and bitter women taking hateful counsel together about the two hall-fires at night,[18] when the sea boomed against the foundations and the wild winter wind was loose over the battlements. And in the study we may reconstruct for ourselves some pale figure of what life then was. Not so when we are there; when we are there such thoughts come to us only to intensify a contrary impression, and association is turned against itself.[19] I remember walking thither three afternoons in succession, my eyes weary with being set against the wind, and how, dropping suddenly over the edge of the down, I found myself in a new world of warmth and shelter. The wind, from which I had escaped, "as from an enemy,"[20] was seemingly quite local. It carried no clouds with it, and came from such a quarter that it did not trouble the sea within view. The two castles, black and ruinous as the rocks about them, were still distinguishable from these by something more insecure and fantastic in the outline, something that the last storm had left imminent and the next would demolish entirely. It would be difficult to render in words the sense of peace that took possession of me on these three afternoons. It was helped out, as I have said, by the contrast. The shore was battered and bemauled by previous tempests; I had the memory at heart of the insane strife of the pigmies who had erected these two castles and lived in them in mutual distrust and enmity, and knew I had only to put my head out of this little cup of shelter to find the hard wind blowing in my eyes; and yet there were the two great tracts of motionless blue air and peaceful sea looking on, unconcerned and apart, at the turmoil of the present moment and the memorials of the precarious past. There is ever something transitory and fretful in the impression of a high wind under a cloudless sky; it seems to have no root in the constitution of things; it must speedily begin to faint and wither away like a cut flower. And on those days the thought of the wind and the thought of human life came very near together in my mind. Our noisy years did indeed seem moments[21] in the being of the eternal silence: and the wind, in the face of that great field of stationary blue, was as the wind of a butterfly's wing. The placidity of the sea was a thing likewise to be remembered. Shelley speaks of the sea as "hungering for calm,"[22] and in this place one learned to understand the phrase. Looking down into these green waters from the broken edge of the rock, or swimming leisurely in the sunshine, it seemed to me that they were enjoying their own tranquillity; and when now and again it was disturbed by a wind ripple on the surface, or the quick black passage of a fish far below, they settled back again (one could fancy) with relief.

On shore, too, in the little nook of shelter, everything was so subdued and still that the least particular struck in me a pleasurable surprise. The desultory crackling of the whin-pods[23] in the afternoon sun usurped the ear. The hot, sweet breath of the bank, that had been saturated all day long with sunshine, and now exhaled it into my face, was like the breath of a fellow-creature. I remember that I was haunted by two lines of French verse; in some dumb way they seemed to fit my surroundings and give expression to the contentment that was in me, and I kept repeating to myself—

"Mon coeur est un luth suspendu,[24]
Sitôt qu'on le touche, il résonne."

I can give no reason why these lines came to me at this time; and for that very cause I repeat them here. For all I know, they may serve to complete the impression in the mind of the reader, as they were certainly a part of it for me.

And this happened to me in the place of all others where I liked least to stay. When I think of it I grow ashamed of my own ingratitude. "Out of the strong came forth sweetness."[25] There, in the bleak and gusty North,

I received, perhaps, my strongest impression of peace. I saw the sea to be great and calm; and the earth, in that little corner, was all alive and friendly to me. So, wherever a man is, he will find something to please and pacify him: in the town he will meet pleasant faces of men and women, and see beautiful flowers at a window, or hear a cage-bird singing at the corner of the gloomiest street; and for the country, there is no country without some amenity—let him only look for it in the right spirit, and he will surely find.

NOTES

This article first appeared in the *Portfolio*, for November 1874, and was not reprinted until two years after Stevenson's death, in 1896, when it was included in the *Miscellanies* (Edinburgh Edition, *Miscellanies*, Vol. IV, pp. 131-142). The editor of the *Portfolio* was the well-known art critic, Philip Gilbert Hamerton (1834-1894), author of the *Intellectual Life* (1873). Just one year before, Stevenson had had printed in the *Portfolio* his first contribution to any periodical, *Roads*. Although *The Enjoyment of Unpleasant Places* attracted scarcely any attention on its first appearance, and has since become practically forgotten, there is perhaps no better essay among his earlier works with which to begin a study of his personality, temperament, and style. In its cheerful optimism this article is particularly characteristic of its author. It should be remembered that when this essay was first printed, Stevenson was only twenty-four years old.

[Note 1: *It is a difficult matter*, etc. The appreciation of nature is a quite modern taste, for although people have always loved the scenery which reminds them of home, it was not at all fashionable in England to love nature for its own sake before 1740. Thomas Gray was the first person in Europe who seems to have exhibited a real love of mountains (see his *Letters*). A study of the development of the appreciation of nature before and after Wordsworth (England's greatest nature poet) is exceedingly interesting. See Myra Reynolds, *The Treatment of Nature in English Poetry between Pope and Wordsworth* (1896).]

[Note 2: *This discipline in scenery.* Note what is said on this subject in Browning's extraordinary poem, *Fra Lippo Lippi*, vs. 300-302.

"For, don't you mark? We're made so that we love
First when we see them painted, things we have passed
Perhaps a hundred times nor cared to see."]

[Note 3: *Brantôme quaintly tells us, "fait des discours en soi pour se soutenir en chemin."* Freely translated, "the traveller talks to himself to keep up his courage on the road." Pierre de Bourdeille, Abbé de Brantôme, (cir. 1534-1614), travelled all over Europe. His works were not published till long after his death, in 1665. Several complete editions of his writings in numerous volumes have appeared in the nineteenth century, one edited by the famous writer, Prosper Mérimée.]

35

[Note 4: *We are provocative of beauty.* Compare again, *Fra Lippo*
Lippi, vs. 215 et seq.

"Or say there's beauty with no soul at all—
(I never saw it—put the case the same—)
If you get simple beauty and nought else,
You get about the best thing God invents:
That's somewhat: and you'll find the soul you have missed,
Within yourself, when you return him thanks."]

[Note 5: *Callot, or Sadeler, or Paul Brill.* Jacques Callot was an eminent French artist of the XVII century, born at Nancy in 1592, died 1635. Matthaeus and Paul Brill were two celebrated Dutch painters. Paul, the younger brother of Matthaeus, was born about 1555, and died in 1626. His development in landscape-painting was remarkable. Gilles Sadeler, born at Antwerp 1570, died at Prague 1629, a famous artist, and nephew of two well-known engravers. He was called the "Phoenix of Engraving."]

[Note 6: *Dick Turpin.* Dick Turpin was born in Essex, England, and was originally a butcher. Afterwards he became a notorious highwayman, and was finally executed for horse-stealing, 10 April 1739. He and his steed Black Bess are well described in W. H. Ainsworth's *Rookwood,* and in his *Ballads.*]

[Note 7: *The Trossachs.* The word means literally, "bristling country." A beautifully romantic tract, beginning immediately to the east of Loch Katrine in Perth, Scotland. Stevenson's statement, "if a man of admirable romantic instinct had not peopled it for them with harmonious figures," refers to Walter Scott, and more particularly to the *Lady of the Lake* (1810).]

[Note 8: *I am happier where it is tame and fertile, and not readily pleased without trees.* Notice the kind of country he begins to describe in the next paragraph. Is there really any contradiction in his statements?]

[Note 9: *Like David before Saul.* David charmed Saul out of his sadness, according to the Biblical story, not with nature, but with music. See I *Samuel* XVI. 14-23. But in Browning's splendid poem, *Saul* (1845), nature and music are combined in David's inspired playing.

"And I first played the tune all our sheep know," etc.]

[Note 10: *The sermon in stones.* See the beginning of the second act of *As You Like It*, where the exiled Duke says,

"And this our life exempt from public haunt
Finds tongues in trees, books in the running brooks,
Sermons in stones and good in everything."

It is not at all certain that Shakspere used the word "sermons" here in the modern sense; he very likely meant merely discourses, conversations.]

[Note 11: *Wuthering Heights.* The well-known novel (1847) by Emily Bronte (1818-1848) sister of the more famous Charlotte Bronte. The "little summer scene" Stevenson mentions, is in Chapter XXIV.]

[Note 12: *A solitary, spectacled stone-breaker.* To the pedestrian or cyclist, no difference between Europe and America is more striking than the comparative excellence of the country roads. The roads in Europe, even in lonely and remote districts, where one may travel for hours without seeing a house, are usually in perfect condition, hard, white and absolutely smooth. The slightest defect or abrasion is immediately repaired by one of these stone-breakers Stevenson mentions, a solitary individual, his eyes concealed behind large green goggles, to protect them from the glare and the flying bits of stone.]

[Note 13: *Ashamed and cold.* An excellent example of what Ruskin called "the pathetic fallacy."]

[Note 14: *The foliage is coloured like foliage in a gale.* Cf. Tennyson, *In Memoriam*, LXXII:—

"With blasts that blow the poplar white."]

[Note 15: *Wordsworth, in a beautiful passage.* The passage Stevenson quotes is in Book VII of *The Prelude*, called *Residence in London*.]

[Note 16: *Cologne Cathedral, the great unfinished marvel by the Rhine.* This great cathedral, generally regarded as the most perfect Gothic church in the world, was begun in 1248, and was not completed
until 1880, seven years after Stevenson wrote this essay.]

[Note 17: *In a golden zone like Apollo's.* The Greek God Apollo, later identified with Helios, the Sun-god. The twin towers of Cologne Cathedral are over 500 feet high, so that the experience described here is quite possible.]

[Note 18: *The two hall-fires at night.* In mediaeval castles, the hall was the general living-room, used regularly for meals, for assemblies, and for all social requirements. The modern word "dining-hall" preserves the old significance of the word. The familiar expression, "bower and hall," is simply, in plain prose, bedroom and sitting-room.]

[Note 19: *Association is turned against itself.* It is seldom that Stevenson uses an expression that is not instantly transparently clear. Exactly what does he mean by this phrase?]

[Note 20: *"As from an enemy."* Alluding to the passage Stevenson has quoted above, from Wordsworth's *Prelude*.]

[Note 21: *Our noisy years did indeed seem moments.* A favorite reflection of Stevenson's, occurring in nearly all his serious essays.]

[Note 22: *Shelley speaks of the sea as "hungering for calm."* This passage occurs in the poem *Prometheus Unbound*, Act III, end of Scene 2.

"Behold the Nereids under the green sea—
Their wavering limbs borne on the wind like stream,
Their white arms lifted o'er their streaming hair,
With garlands pied and starry sea-flower crowns,—
Hastening to grace their mighty Sister's joy.
It is the unpastured sea hungering for calm."]

[Note 23: *Whin-pods.* "Whin" is from the Welsh *çwyn*, meaning "weed." Whin is gorse or furze, and the sound Stevenson alludes to is frequently heard in Scotland.]

[Note 24: "*Mon coeur est un luth suspendu.*" These beautiful words are from the poet Béranger (1780-1857). It is probable that Stevenson found them first not in the original, but in reading the tales of Poe, for the "two lines of French verse" that "haunted" Stevenson are quoted by Poe at the beginning of one of his most famous pieces, *The Fall of the House of Usher*, where, however, the third, and not the first person is used:—

"*Son* coeur est un luth suspendu;
Sitôt qu'on le touche il résonne."]

[Note 25: "*Out of the strong came forth sweetness.*" Alluding to the riddle propounded by Samson. See the book of *Judges*, Chapter XIV.]

II

AN APOLOGY FOR IDLERS

BOSWELL: "We grow weary when idle."

JOHNSON: "That is, sir, because others being busy, we want company; but if we were idle, there would be no growing weary; we should all entertain one another."[1]

Just now, when every one is bound, under pain of a decree in absence convicting them of *lèse*-respectability,[2] to enter on some lucrative profession, and labour therein with something not far short of enthusiasm, a cry from the opposite party who are content when they have enough, and like to look on and enjoy in the meanwhile, savours a little of bravado and gasconade.[3] And yet this should not be. Idleness so called, which does not consist in doing nothing, but in doing a great deal not recognised in the dogmatic formularies of the ruling class, has as good a right to state its position as industry itself. It is admitted that the presence of people who refuse to enter in the great handicap race for sixpenny pieces, is at once an insult and a disenchantment for those who do. A fine fellow (as we see so many) takes his determination, votes for the sixpences, and in the emphatic Americanism, "goes for" them.[4] And while such an one is ploughing distressfully up the road, it is not hard to understand his resentment, when he perceives cool persons in the meadows by the wayside, lying with a handkerchief over their ears and a glass at their elbow. Alexander is touched in a very delicate place by the disregard of Diogenes.[5] Where was the glory of having taken Rome[6] for these tumultuous barbarians, who poured into the Senate house, and found the Fathers sitting silent and unmoved by their success? It is a sore thing to have laboured along and scaled the arduous hilltops, and when all is done, find humanity indifferent to your achievement. Hence physicists condemn the unphysical; financiers have only a superficial toleration for those who know little of stocks; literary persons despise the unlettered; and people of all pursuits combine to disparage those who have none.

But though this is one difficulty of the subject, it is not the greatest. You could not be put in prison for speaking against industry, but you can be sent to Coventry[7] for speaking like a fool. The greatest difficulty with most subjects is to do them well; therefore, please to remember this is an apology. It is certain that much may be judiciously argued in favour of diligence; only there is something to be said against it, and that is what, on the present occasion, I have to say. To state one argument is not necessarily to be deaf to all others, and that a man has written a book of travels in Montenegro, is no reason why he should never have been to Richmond.[8]

It is surely beyond a doubt that people should be a good deal idle in youth. For though here and there a Lord Macaulay may escape from school honours[9] with all his wits about him, most boys pay so dear for their medals that they never afterwards have a shot in their locker, "and begin the world bankrupt." And the same holds true during all the time a lad is educating himself, or suffering others to educate him. It must have been a very foolish old gentleman who addressed Johnson at Oxford in these words: "Young man, ply your book diligently now, and acquire a stock of knowledge; for when years come upon you, you will find that poring upon books will be but an irksome task." The old gentleman seems to have been unaware that many other things besides reading grow irksome, and not a few become impossible, by the time a man has to use spectacles and cannot walk without a stick. Books are good enough in their own way, but they are a mighty bloodless substitute for life. It seems a pity to sit, like the Lady of Shalott,[10] peering into a mirror, with your back turned on all the bustle and glamour of reality. And if a man reads very hard, as the old anecdote reminds us, he will have little time for thoughts.

If you look back on your own education, I am sure it will not be the full, vivid, instructive hours of truantry that you regret; you would rather cancel some lack-lustre periods between sleep and waking[11] in the class. For my own part, I have attended a good many lectures in my time.

I still remember that the spinning of a top is a case of Kinetic Stability. I still remember that Emphyteusis is not a disease, nor Stillicide[12] a crime. But though I would not willingly part with such scraps of science, I do not set the same store by them as by certain other odds and ends that I came by in the open street while I was playing truant. This is not the moment to dilate on that mighty place of education, which was the favourite school of Dickens and of Balzac,[13] and turns out yearly many inglorious masters in the Science of the Aspects of Life. Suffice it to say this: if a lad does not learn in the streets, it is because he has no faculty of learning. Nor is the truant always in the streets, for if he prefers, he may go out by the gardened suburbs into the country. He may pitch on some tuft of lilacs over a burn, and smoke innumerable pipes to the tune of the water on the stones. A bird will sing in the thicket. And there he may fall into a vein of kindly thought, and see things in a new perspective. Why, if this be not education, what is? We may conceive Mr. Worldly Wiseman[14] accosting such an one, and the conversation that should thereupon ensue:—

"How, now, young fellow, what dost thou here?"

"Truly, sir, I take mine ease."

"Is not this the hour of the class? and should'st thou not be plying thy Book with diligence, to the end thou mayest obtain knowledge?"

"Nay, but thus also I follow after Learning, by your leave."

"Learning, quotha! After what fashion, I pray thee? Is it mathematics?"

"No, to be sure."

"Is it metaphysics?"

"Nor that."

"Is it some language?"

"Nay, it is no language."

"Is it a trade?"

"Nor a trade neither."

"Why, then, what is't?"

"Indeed, sir, as a time may soon come for me to go upon Pilgrimage, I am desirous to note what is commonly done by persons in my case, and where are the ugliest Sloughs and Thickets on the Road; as also, what manner of Staff is of the best service. Moreover, I lie here, by this water, to learn by root-of-heart a lesson which my master teaches me to call Peace, or Contentment."

Hereupon, Mr. Worldly Wiseman was much commoved with passion, and shaking his cane with a very threatful countenance, broke forth upon this wise: "Learning, quotha!" said he; "I would have all such rogues scourged by the Hangman!"

And so he would go his way, ruffling out his cravat with a crackle of starch, like a turkey when it spread its feathers.

Now this, of Mr. Wiseman, is the common opinion. A fact is not called a fact, but a piece of gossip, if it does not fall into one of your scholastic categories. An inquiry must be in some acknowledged direction, with a name to go by; or else you are not inquiring at all, only lounging; and the workhouse is too good for you. It is supposed that all knowledge is at the bottom of a well, or the far end of a telescope. Sainte-Beuve,[15] as he grew older, came to regard all experience as a single great book, in which to study for a few years ere we go hence; and it seemed all one to him whether you should read in Chapter xx., which is the differential calculus, or in Chapter xxxix., which is hearing the band play in the gardens. As a matter of fact, an intelligent person, looking out of his eyes and hearkening in his ears, with a smile on his face all the time, will get more true education than many another in a life of heroic vigils. There is certainly some chill and arid knowledge to be found upon the summits of formal and laborious science; but it is all round about you, and for the trouble of looking, that you will acquire the warm and palpitating facts of life. While others are filling their memory with a lumber of words, one-half of which they will forget before the week be out, your truant may learn some really useful art: to play the fiddle, to know a good cigar, or to speak with ease and opportunity to all varieties of men. Many who have "plied their book diligently," and know all about some one branch or another of accepted lore, come out of the study with an ancient and owl-like demeanour, and prove dry, stockish, and dyspeptic in all the better and brighter parts of life. Many make a large fortune, who remain underbred and pathetically stupid to the last. And meantime there goes the idler, who began life along with them—by your leave, a different picture. He has had time to take care of his health and his spirits; he has been a great deal in the open air, which is the most salutary of all things for both body and mind; and if he has never read the great Book in very recondite places, he has dipped into it and skimmed it over to excellent purpose. Might not the student afford some Hebrew roots, and the business man some of his half-crowns, for a share of the idler's knowledge of life at large, and Art of Living? Nay, and the idler has another and more important quality than these. I mean his wisdom. He who has much looked on at the childish satisfaction of other people in their hobbies, will regard his own with only a very ironical indulgence. He will not be heard among the dogmatists. He will have a great and cool allowance for all sorts of people and opinions. If he finds no out-of-the-way truths, he will identify himself with no very burning falsehood. His way took him along a by-road, not much frequented, but very even and pleasant, which is called Commonplace Lane, and leads to the Belvedere of Commonsense.[16] Thence he shall command an agreeable, if no very noble prospect; and while others behold the East and West, the Devil and the Sunrise, he will be contentedly aware of a sort of morning hour upon all sublunary things, with an army of shadows running speedily and in many different directions into the great daylight of Eternity. The shadows and the generations, the shrill doctors and the plangent wars,[17] go by into ultimate silence and emptiness; but underneath all this, a man may see, out of the Belvedere windows, much green and peaceful landscape; many firelit parlours; good people laughing, drinking, and making love as they did before the Flood or the French Revolution; and the old shepherd[18] telling his tale under the hawthorn.

Extreme *busyness*, whether at school or college, kirk or market, is a symptom of deficient vitality; and a faculty for idleness implies a catholic appetite and a strong sense of personal identity. There is a sort of dead-alive, hackneyed people about, who are scarcely conscious of living except in the exercise of some conventional occupation. Bring these fellows into the country, or set them aboard ship, and you will see how they pine for their desk or their study. They have no curiosity; they cannot give themselves over to random provocations; they do not take pleasure in the exercise of their faculties for its own sake; and unless Necessity lays about them with a stick, they will even stand still. It is no good speaking to such folk: they *cannot* be idle, their nature is not generous enough; and they pass those hours in a sort of coma, which are not dedicated to furious moiling in the gold-mill. When they do not require to go to the office, when they are not hungry and have no mind to drink, the whole breathing world is a blank to them. If they have to wait an hour or so for a train, they fall into a stupid trance with their eyes open. To see them, you would suppose there was nothing to look at and no one to speak with; you would imagine they were paralysed or alienated; and yet very possibly they are hard workers in their own way, and have good eyesight for a flaw in a deed or a turn of the market. They have been to school and college, but all the time they had their eye on the medal; they have gone about in the world and mixed with clever people, but all the time they were thinking of their own affairs. As if a man's soul were not too small to begin with, they have dwarfed and narrowed theirs by a life of all work and no play; until here they are at forty, with a listless attention, a mind vacant of all material of amusement, and not one thought to rub against another, while they wait for the train. Before he was breeched, he might have clambered on the boxes; when he was twenty, he would have stared at the girls; but now the pipe is smoked out, the snuffbox empty, and my gentleman sits bolt upright upon a bench, with lamentable eyes. This does not appeal to me as being Success in Life.

But it is not only the person himself who suffers from his busy habits, but his wife and children, his friends and relations, and down to the very people he sits with in a railway carriage or an omnibus. Perpetual devotion to what a man calls his business, is only to be sustained by perpetual neglect of many other things. And it is not by any means certain that a man's business is the most important thing he has to do. To an impartial estimate it will seem clear that many of the wisest, most virtuous, and most beneficent parts that are to be played upon the Theatre of Life are filled by gratuitous performers, and pass, among the world at large, as phases of idleness. For in that Theatre not only the walking gentlemen, singing chambermaids, and diligent fiddlers in the orchestra, but those who look on and clap their hands from the benches, do really play a part and fulfil important offices towards the general result. You are no doubt very dependent on the care of your lawyer and stockbroker, of the guards and signalmen who convey you rapidly from place to place, and the policemen who walk the streets for your protection; but is there not a thought of gratitude in your heart for certain other benefactors who set you smiling when they fall in your way, or season your dinner with good company? Colonel Newcome helped to lose his friend's money; Fred Bayham had an ugly trick of borrowing shirts; and yet they were better people to fall among than Mr. Barnes. And though Falstaff was neither sober nor very honest, I think I could name one or two long-faced Barabbases whom the world could better have done without. Hazlitt mentions that he was more sensible of obligation to

Northcote,[19] who had never done him anything he could call a service, than to his whole circle of ostentatious friends; for he thought a good companion emphatically the greatest benefactor. I know there are people in the world who cannot feel grateful unless the favour has been done them at the cost of pain and difficulty. But this is a churlish disposition. A man may send you six sheets of letter-paper covered with the most entertaining gossip, or you may pass half an hour pleasantly, perhaps profitably, over an article of his; do you think the service would be greater, if he had made the manuscript in his heart's blood, like a compact with the devil? Do you really fancy you should be more beholden to your correspondent, if he had been damning you all the while for your importunity? Pleasures are more beneficial than duties because, like the quality of mercy,[20] they are not strained, and they are twice blest. There must always be two to a kiss, and there may be a score in a jest; but wherever there is an element of sacrifice, the favour is conferred with pain, and, among generous people, received with confusion. There is no duty we so much underrate as the duty of being happy. By being happy, we sow anonymous benefits upon the world, which remain unknown even to ourselves, or when they are disclosed, surprise nobody so much as the benefactor. The other day, a ragged, barefoot boy ran down the street after a marble, with so jolly an air that he set every one he passed into a good humour; one of these persons, who had been delivered from more than usually black thoughts, stopped the little fellow and gave him some money with this remark: "You see what sometimes comes of looking pleased." If he had looked pleased before, he had now to look both pleased and mystified. For my part, I justify this encouragement of smiling rather than tearful children; I do not wish to pay for tears anywhere but upon the stage; but I am prepared to deal largely in the opposite commodity. A happy man or woman is a better thing to find than a five-pound note. He or she is a radiating focus of good-will; and their entrance into a room is as though another candle had been lighted. We need not care whether they could prove the forty-seventh proposition; they do a better thing than that, they practically demonstrate the great Theorum of the liveableness of Life. Consequently, if a person cannot be happy without remaining idle, idle he should remain. It is a revolutionary precept; but thanks to hunger and the workhouse, one not easily to be abused; and within practical limits, it is one of the most incontestable truths in the whole Body of Morality. Look at one of your industrious fellows for a moment, I beseech you. He sows hurry and reaps indigestion; he puts a vast deal of activity out to interest, and receives a large measure of nervous derangement in return. Either he absents himself entirely from all fellowship, and lives a recluse in a garret, with carpet slippers and a leaden inkpot; or he comes among people swiftly and bitterly, in a contraction of his whole nervous system, to discharge some temper before he returns to work. I do not care how much or how well he works, this fellow is an evil feature in other people's lives. They would be happier if he were dead. They could easier do without his services in the Circumlocution Office, than they can tolerate his fractious spirits. He poisons life at the well-head. It is better to be beggared out of hand by a scapegrace nephew, than daily hag-ridden by a peevish uncle.

And what, in God's name, is all this pother about? For what cause do they embitter their own and other people's lives? That a man should publish three or thirty articles a year, that he should finish or not finish his great allegorical picture, are questions of little interest to the world. The ranks of life are full; and although a thousand fall, there are always some to go into the breach. When they told Joan of Arc[21] she should be at home minding women's work, she answered there were plenty to spin and wash. And so, even with your own rare gifts! When nature is "so careless of the single life,"[22] why should we coddle ourselves into the fancy that our own is of exceptional importance? Suppose Shakespeare had been knocked on the head some dark night in Sir Thomas Lucy's[23] preserves, the world would have wagged on better or worse, the pitcher gone to the well, the scythe to the corn, and the student to his book; and no one been any the wiser of the loss. There are not many works extant, if you look the alternative all over, which are worth the price of a pound of tobacco to a man of limited means. This is a sobering reflection for the proudest of our earthly vanities. Even a tobacconist may, upon consideration, find no great cause for personal vainglory in the phrase; for although tobacco is an admirable sedative, the qualities necessary for retailing it are neither rare nor precious in themselves. Alas and alas! you may take it how you will, but the services of no single individual are indispensable. Atlas[24] was just a gentleman with a protracted nightmare! And yet you see merchants who go and labour themselves into a great fortune and thence into bankruptcy court; scribblers who keep scribbling at little articles until their temper is a cross to all who come about them, as though Pharaoh should set the Israelites to make a pin instead of a pyramid;[25] and fine young men who work themselves into a decline,[26] and are driven off in a hearse with white plumes upon it. Would you not suppose these persons had been whispered, by the Master of the Ceremonies, the promise of some momentous destiny? and that this lukewarm bullet on which they play their farces was the bull's-eye and centrepoint of all the universe? And yet it is not so. The ends for which they give away their priceless youth, for all they know, may be chimerical or hurtful; the glory and riches they expect may never come, or may find them indifferent; and they and the world they inhabit are so inconsiderable that the mind freezes at the thought.

NOTES

This essay was first printed in the *Cornhill Magazine*, for July 1877, Vol. XXXVI, pp. 80-86. It was next published in the volume, *Virginibus Puerisque*, in 1881. Although this book contains some of the most admirable specimens of Stevenson's style, it did not have a large sale, and it was not until 1887 that another edition Appeared. The editor of the *Cornhill Magazine* from 1871 to 1882 was Leslie Stephen (1832-1904), whose kindness and encouragement to the new writer were of the utmost importance at this critical time. That so grave and serious a critic as Leslie Stephen should have taken such delight in a *jeu d'esprit* like *Idlers*, is proof, if any were needed, for the breadth of his literary outlook. Stevenson had been at work on this article a year before its appearance, which shows that his *Apology for Idlers* demanded from him anything but idling. As Graham Balfour says, in his *Life of Stevenson*, I, 122, "Except before his own conscience, there was hardly any time when the author of the *Apology for Idlers* ever really neglected the tasks of his true vocation." In July 1876 he wrote to Mrs. Sitwell, "A paper called 'A Defence of Idlers' (which is really a defence of R.L.S.) is in a good way." A year later, after the publication of the article, he wrote (in August 1877) to Sidney Colvin, "Stephen has written to me apropos of 'Idlers,' that something more in that vein would be agreeable to his views. From Stephen I count that a devil of a lot." It is noteworthy that this charming essay had been refused by

Macmillan's Magazine before Stephen accepted it for the *Cornhill.* (*Life,* I, 180).

[Note 1: The conversation between Boswell and Johnson, quoted at the beginning of the essay, occurred on the 26 October 1769, at the famous Mitre Tavern. In Stevenson's quotation, the word "all" should be inserted after the word "were" to correspond with the original text, and to make sense. Johnson, though constitutionally lazy, was no defender of Idlers, and there is a sly humour in Stevenson's appealing to him as authority. Boswell says in his *Life,* under date of 1780, "He would allow no settled indulgence of idleness upon principle, and always repelled every attempt to urge excuses for it. A friend one day suggested, that it was not wholesome to study soon after dinner. JOHNSON: 'Ah, sir, don't give way to such a fancy. At one time of my life I had taken it into my head that it was not wholesome to study between breakfast and dinner.'"]

[Note 2: *Lèse-respectability.* From the French verb *leser,* to hurt, to injure. The most common employment of this verb is in the phrase "*lèse-majesté,*" high treason. Stevenson's mood here is like that of Lowell, when he said regretfully, speaking of the eighteenth century, "Responsibility for the universe had not then been invented." (*Essay on Gray.*)]

[Note 3: *Gasconade.* Boasting. The inhabitants of Gascony (*Gascogne*) a province in the south-west of France, are proverbial not only for their impetuosity and courage, but for their willingness to brag of the possession of these qualities. Excellent examples of the typical Gascon in literature are D'Artagnan in Dumas's *Trois Mousquetaires* (1844) and Cyrano in Rostand's splendid drama, *Cyrano de Bergerac* (1897).]

[Note 4: *In the emphatic Americanism, "goes for" them.* When Stevenson wrote this (1876-77), he had not yet been in America. Two years later, in 1879, when he made the journey across the plains, he had many opportunities to record Americanisms far more emphatic than the harmless phrase quoted here, which can hardly be called an Americanism. Murray's *New English Dictionary* gives excellent English examples of this particular sense of "go for" in the years 1641, 1790, 1864, and 1882!]

[Note 5: *Alexander is touched in a very delicate place.* Alluding to the famous interview between the young Alexander and the old Diogenes, which took place at Corinth about 330 B.C. Alexander asked Diogenes in what way he could be of service to him, and the philosopher replied gruffly, "By standing out of my sunshine." As a young man Diogenes had been given to all excesses of dissipation; but he later went to the opposite extreme of asceticism, being one of the earliest and most striking illustrations of "plain living and high thinking." The debauchery of his youth and the privation and exposure of his old age did not deeply affect his hardy constitution, for he is said to have lived to the age of ninety. In the charming play by the Elizabethan, John Lyly, *A moste excellente Comedie of Alexander, Campaspe, and Diogenes* (1584), the conversations between the man who has conquered the world and the man who has overcome the world are highly entertaining.]

[Note 6: *Where was the glory of having taken Rome.* This refers to the invasion by the Gauls about the year 389 B. C. A good account is given in T. Arnold's *History of Rome* I, pp. 534 et seq.]

[Note 7: *Sent to Coventry.* The origin of this proverb, which means of course, "to ostracise," probably dates back to 1647, when, according to Clarendon's *History of the Great Rebellion*, VI, par. 83, Royalist prisoners were sent to the parliamentary stronghold of Coventry, in Warwickshire.]

[Note 8: *Montenegro ... Richmond.* Montenegro is one of the smallest principalities in the world, about 3,550 square miles. It is in the Balkan peninsula, to the east of the lower Adriatic, between Austro-Hungary and Turkey. When Stevenson was writing this essay, 1876-77, Montenegro was the subject of much discussion, owing to the part she took in the Russo-Turkish war. The year after this article was published (1878) Montenegro reached the coast of the Adriatic for the first time, and now has two tiny seaports. Tennyson celebrated the hardy virtues of the inhabitants in his sonnet *Montenegro*, written in 1877.

"O smallest among peoples! rough rock-throne
Of Freedom! warriors beating back the swarm
Of Turkish Islam for five hundred years."

Richmond is on the river Thames, close to the city of London.]

[Note 9: *Lord Macaulay may escape from school honours.* Stevenson here alludes to the oft-heard statement that the men who succeed in after life have generally been near the foot of their classes at school and college. It is impossible to prove either the falsity or truth of so general a remark, but it is easier to point out men who have been successful both at school and in life, than to find sufficient evidence that school and college prizes prevent further triumphs. Macaulay, who is noted by Stevenson as an exception, was precocious enough to arouse the fears rather than the hopes of his friends. When he was four years old, he hurt his finger, and a lady inquiring politely as to whether the injured member was better, the infant replied gravely, "Thank you, Madam, the agony is abated."]

[Note 10: *The Lady of Shalott*. See Tennyson's beautiful poem (1833).

"And moving thro' a mirror clear
That hangs before her all the year,
Shadows of the world appear."]

[Note 11: *Some lack-lustre periods between sleep and waking.* Cf. *King Lear*, Act I, Sc. 2, vs. 15. "Got 'tween asleep and wake."]

[Note 12: _Kinetic Stability ... *Emphyteusis* ... *Stillicide* For Kinetic Stability, see any modern textbook on Physics. *Emphyteusis* is the legal renting of ground; *Stillicide*, a continual dropping of water, as from the eaves of a house. These words, *Emphyteusis* and *Stillicide*, are terms in Roman Law. Stevenson is of course making fun of the required studies of Physics and Roman Law, and of their lack of practical value to him in his chosen career.]

[Note 13: *The favourite school of Dickens and of Balzac.* The great English novelist Dickens (1812-1870) and his greater French contemporary Balzac (1799-1850), show in their works that their chief school was Life.]

[Note 14: *Mr. Worldly Wiseman.* The character in Bunyan's *Pilgrim's Progress* (1678), who meets Christian soon after his setting out from the City of Destruction. *Pilgrim's Progress* was a favorite book of Stevenson's; he alludes to it frequently in his essays. See also his own article *Bagster's Pilgrim's Progress*, first published in the *Magazine of Art* in February 1882. This essay is well worth reading, and the copies of the pictures which he includes are extremely diverting.]

[Note 15: *Sainte-Beuve.* The French writer Sainte-Beuve (1804-1869) is usually regarded today as the greatest literary critic who ever lived. His constant change of convictions enabled him to see life from all sides.]

[Note 16: *Belvedere of Commonsense.* Belvedere is an Italian word, which referred originally to a place of observation on the top of a house, from which one might enjoy an extensive prospect. A portion of the Vatican in Rome is called the Belvedere, thus lending this name to the famous statue of Apollo, which stands there. On the continent, anything like a summer-house is often called a Belvedere. One of the most interesting localities which bears this name is the Belvedere just outside of Weimar, in Germany, where Goethe used to act in his own dramas in the open air theatre.]

[Note 17: *The plangent wars.* Plangent is from the Latin *plango*, to strike, to beat. Stevenson's use of the word is rather unusual in English.]

[Note 18: *The old shepherd telling his tale.*. See Milton, *L'Allegro:*—

"And every shepherd tells his tale
Under the hawthorn in the dale."

"Tells his tale" means of course "counts his sheep," not "tells a story." The old use of the word "tell" for "count" survives to-day in the word "teller" in a parliamentary assemblage, or in a bank.]

[Note 19: *Colonel Newcome ... Fred Bayham ... Mr. Barnes ... Falstaff ... Barabbases ... Hazlitt ... Northcote.* Colonel Newcome, the great character in Thackeray's *The Newcomes* (1854). *Fred Bayham* and *Barnes Newcome* are persons in the same story. One of the best essays on Falstaff is the one printed in the first series of Mr. Augustine Birrell's *Obiter Dicta* (1884). This essay would have pleased Thackeray. One of the finest epitaphs in literature is that pronounced over the supposedly dead body of Falstaff by Prince Hal—"I could have better spared a better man." (*King Henry IV*, Part I, Act V, Sc. 4.) *Barabbas* was the robber who was released at the time of the trial of Christ.... *William Hazlitt* (1778-1830), the well-known essayist, published in 1830 the *Conversations* of *James Northcote* (1746-1831). Northcote was an artist and writer, who had been an assistant in the studio of Sir Joshua Reynolds. Stevenson projected a *Life of Hazlitt*, but later abandoned the undertaking. (*Life,* I, 230.)]

[Note 20: *The quality of mercy.* See Portia's wonderful speech in the *Merchant of Venice*, Act IV, Scene I.]

[Note 21: *Joan of Arc*. The famous inspired French peasant girl, who led the armies of her king to victory, and who was burned at Rouen in 1431. She was variously regarded as a harlot and a saint. In Shakspere's historical plays, she is represented in the basest manner, from conventional motives of English patriotism. Voltaire's scandalous work, *La Pucelle*, and Schiller's noble *Jungfrau von Orleans* make an instructive contrast. She has been the subject of many dramas and works of poetry and fiction. Her latest prominent admirer is Mark Twain, whose historical romance *Joan of Arc* is one of the most carefully written, though not one of the most characteristic of his books.]

[Note 22: "*So careless of the single life*." See Tennyson's *In Memoriam*, LV, where the poet discusses the pessimism caused by regarding the apparent indifference of nature to the happiness of the individual.

"Are God and Nature then at strife,

That Nature lends such evil dreams?

So careful of the type she seems,

So careless of the single life."]

[Note 23: *Shakespeare … Sir Thomas Lucy*. The familiar tradition that Shakspere as a boy was a poacher on the preserves of his aristocratic neighbor, Sir Thomas Lucy. See Halliwell-Phillipps's *Outlines of the Life of Shakespeare*. In 1879, at the first performance of *As You Like It* at the Stratford Memorial Theatre, the deer brought on the stage in Act IV, Scene 2, had been shot that very morning by H.S. Lucy, Esq., of Charlecote Park, a descendant of the owner of the herd traditionally attacked by the future dramatist.]

[Note 24: *Atlas.* In mythology, the leader of the Titans, who fought the Gods, and was condemned by Zeus to carry the weight of the vault of heaven on his head and hands. In the sixteenth century the name Atlas was given to a collection of maps by Mercator, probably because a picture of Atlas had been commonly placed on the title-pages of geographical works.]

[Note 25: *Pharaoh ... Pyramid.* For *Pharaoh's* experiences with the Israelites, see the book of *Exodus.* Pharaoh was merely the name given by the children of Israel to the rulers of Egypt: cf. Caesar, Kaiser, etc. ... The Egyptian pyramids were regarded as one of the seven wonders of ancient times, the great pyramid weighing over six million tons. The pyramids were used for the tombs of monarchs.]

[Note 26: *Young men who work themselves into a decline.* Compare the tone of the close of this essay with that of the conclusion of *AEs Triplex.* Stevenson himself died in the midst of the most arduous work possible—the making of a literary masterpiece.]

III

AES TRIPLEX[1]

The changes wrought by death are in themselves so sharp and final, and so terrible and melancholy in their consequences, that the thing stands alone in man's experience, and has no parallel upon earth. It outdoes all other accidents because it is the last of them. Sometimes it leaps suddenly upon its victims, like a Thug;[2] sometimes it lays a regular siege and creeps upon their citadel during a score of years. And when the business is done, there is sore havoc made in other people's lives, and a pin knocked out by which many subsidiary friendships hung together. There are empty chairs, solitary walks, and single beds at night. Again in taking away our friends, death does not take them away utterly, but leaves behind a mocking, tragical, and soon intolerable residue, which must be hurriedly concealed. Hence a whole chapter of sights and customs striking to the mind, from the pyramids of Egypt to the gibbets and dule trees[3] of mediaeval Europe. The poorest persons have a bit of pageant going towards the tomb; memorial stones are set up over the least memorable; and, in order to preserve some show of respect for what remains of our old loves and friendships, we must accompany it with much grimly ludicrous ceremonial,

64

and the hired undertaker parades before the door. All this, and much more of the same sort, accompanied by the eloquence of poets, has gone a great way to put humanity in error; nay, in many philosophies the error has been embodied and laid down with every circumstance of logic; although in real life the bustle and swiftness, in leaving people little time to think, have not left them time enough to go dangerously wrong in practice.

As a matter of fact, although few things are spoken of with more fearful whisperings than this prospect of death, few have less influence on conduct under healthy circumstances. We have all heard of cities in South America built upon the side of fiery mountains, and how, even in this tremendous neighbourhood, the inhabitants are not a jot more impressed by the solemnity of mortal conditions than if they were delving gardens in the greenest corner of England. There are serenades and suppers and much gallantry among the myrtles overhead; and meanwhile the foundation shudders underfoot, the bowels of the mountain growl, and at any moment living ruin may leap sky-high into the moonlight, and tumble man and his merry-making in the dust. In the eyes of very young people, and very dull old ones, there is something indescribably reckless and desperate in such a picture. It seems not credible that respectable married people, with umbrellas, should find appetite for a bit of supper within quite a long distance of a fiery mountain; ordinary life begins to smell of high-handed debauch when it is carried on so close to a catastrophe; and even cheese and salad, it seems, could hardly be relished in such circumstances without something like a defiance of the Creator. It should be a place for nobody but hermits dwelling in prayer and maceration, or mere born-devils drowning care in a perpetual carouse.

And yet, when one comes to think upon it calmly, the situation of these South American citizens forms only a very pale figure for the state of ordinary mankind. This world itself, travelling blindly and swiftly in overcrowded space, among a million other worlds travelling blindly and swiftly in contrary directions, may very well come by a knock that would set it into explosion like a penny squib. And what, pathologically looked at, is the human body with all its organs, but a mere bagful of petards? The least of these is as dangerous to the whole economy as the ship's powder-magazine to the ship; and with every breath we breathe, and every meal we eat, we are putting one or more of them in peril. If we clung as devotedly as some philosophers pretend we do to the abstract idea of life, or were half as frightened as they make out we are, for the subversive accident that ends it all, the trumpets might sound[4] by the hour and no one would follow them into battle—the blue-peter might fly at the truck,[5] but who would climb into a sea-going ship? Think (if these philosophers were right) with what a preparation of spirit we should affront the daily peril of the dinner-table: a deadlier spot than any battlefield in history, where the far greater proportion of our ancestors have miserably left their bones! What woman would ever be lured into marriage, so much more dangerous than the wildest sea? And what would it be to grow old? For, after a certain distance, every step we take in life we find the ice growing thinner below our feet, and all around us and behind us we see our contemporaries going through. By the time a man gets well into the seventies, his continued existence is a mere miracle; and when he lays his old bones in bed for the night, there is an overwhelming probability that he will never see the day. Do the old men mind it, as a matter of fact? Why, no. They were never merrier; they have their grog at night, and tell the raciest stories; they hear of the death of people about their own age, or even younger, not as if it was a grisly warning, but with a simple childlike pleasure at having outlived someone else; and when a draught might puff them out like a fluttering candle, or a bit of a stumble shatter them like so much glass, their old hearts keep sound and unaffrighted, and they go on, bubbling with laughter, through years of man's age compared to which the valley at Balaclava[6] was as safe and peaceful as a village cricket-green on Sunday. It may fairly be questioned (if we look to the peril only) whether it was a much more daring feat for Curtius[7] to plunge into the gulf, than for any old gentleman of ninety to doff his clothes and clamber into bed.

Indeed, it is a memorable subject for consideration, with what unconcern and gaiety mankind pricks on along the Valley of the Shadow of Death. The whole way is one wilderness of snares, and the end of it, for those who fear the last pinch, is irrevocable ruin. And yet we go spinning through it all, like a party for the Derby.[8] Perhaps the reader remembers one of the humorous devices of the deified Caligula:[9] how he encouraged a vast concourse of holiday-makers on to his bridge over Baiae[10] bay; and when they were in the height of their enjoyment, turned loose the Praetorian guards[11] among the company, and had them tossed into the sea. This is no bad miniature of the dealings of nature with the transitory race of man. Only, what a chequered picnic we have of it, even while it lasts! and into what great waters, not to be crossed by any swimmer, God's pale Praetorian throws us over in the end!

We live the time that a match flickers; we pop the cork of a ginger-beer bottle, and the earthquake swallows us on the instant. Is it not odd, is it not incongruous, is it not, in the highest sense of human speech, incredible, that we should think so highly of the ginger-beer, and regard so little the devouring earthquake? The love of Life and the fear of Death are two famous phrases that grow harder to understand the more we think about them. It is a well-known fact that an immense proportion of boat accidents would never happen if people held the sheet in their hands instead of making it fast; and yet, unless it be some martinet of a professional mariner or some landsman with shattered nerves, every one of God's creatures makes it fast. A strange instance of man's unconcern and brazen boldness in the face of death!

We confound ourselves with metaphysical phrases, which we import into daily talk with noble inappropriateness. We have no idea of what death is, apart from its circumstances and some of its consequences to others; and although we have some experience of living, there is not a man on earth who has flown so high into abstraction as to have any practical guess at the meaning of the Word *life*. All literature, from Job and Omar Khayyam to Thomas Carlyle or Walt Whitman,[12] is but an attempt to look upon the human state with such largeness of view as shall enable us to rise from the consideration of living to the Definition of Life. And our sages give us about the best satisfaction in their power when they say that it is a vapour, or a show, or made out of the same stuff with dreams.[13] Philosophy, in its more rigid sense, has been at the same work for ages; and after a myriad bald heads have wagged over the problem, and piles of words have been heaped one upon another into dry and cloudy volumes without end, philosophy has the honour of laying before us, with modest pride, her contribution towards the subject: that life is a Permanent Possibility of Sensation.[14]

Truly a fine result! A man may very well love beef, or hunting, or a woman; but surely, surely, not a Permanent Possibility of Sensation. He may be afraid of a precipice, or a dentist, or a large enemy with a club, or even an undertaker's man; but not certainly of abstract death. We may trick with the word life in its dozen senses until we are weary of tricking; we may argue in terms of all the philosophies on earth, but one fact remains true throughout—that we do not love life, in the sense that we are greatly preoccupied about its conservation; that we do not, properly speaking, love life at all, but living. Into the views of the least careful there will enter some degree of providence; no man's eyes are fixed entirely on the passing hour; but although we have some anticipation of good health, good weather, wine, active employment, love, and self-approval, the sum of these anticipations does not amount to anything like a general view of life's possibilities and issues; nor are those who cherish them most vividly, at all the most scrupulous of their personal safety. To be deeply interested in the accidents of our existence, to enjoy keenly the mixed texture of human experience, rather leads a man to disregard precautions, and risk his neck against a straw. For surely the love of living is stronger in an Alpine climber roping over a peril, or a hunter riding merrily at a stiff fence, than in a creature who lives upon a diet and walks a measured distance in the interest of his constitution.

There is a great deal of very vile nonsense talked upon both sides of the matter: tearing divines reducing life to the dimensions of a mere funeral procession, so short as to be hardly decent; and melancholy unbelievers yearning for the tomb as if it were a world too far away. Both sides must feel a little ashamed of their performances now and again when they draw in their chairs to dinner. Indeed, a good meal and a bottle of wine is an answer to most standard works upon the question. When a man's heart warms to his viands, he forgets a great deal of sophistry, and soars into a rosy zone of contemplation. Death may be knocking at the door, like the Commander's statue;[15] we have something else in hand, thank God, and let him knock. Passing bells are ringing all the world over. All the world over, and every hour,[16] someone is parting company with all his aches and ecstasies. For us also the trap is laid. But we are so fond of life that we have no leisure to entertain the terror of death. It is a honeymoon with us all through, and none of the longest. Small blame to us if we give our whole hearts to this glowing bride of ours, to the appetites, to honour, to the hungry curiosity of the mind, to the pleasure of the eyes in nature, and the pride of our own nimble bodies.

We all of us appreciate the sensations; but as for caring about the Permanence of the Possibility, a man's head is generally very bald, and his senses very dull, before he comes to that. Whether we regard life as a lane leading to a dead wall—a mere bag's end,[17] as the French say—or whether we think of it as a vestibule or gymnasium, where we wait our turn and prepare our faculties for some more noble destiny; whether we thunder in a pulpit, or pule in little atheistic poetry-books, about its vanity and brevity; whether we look justly for years of health and vigour, or are about to mount into a Bath-chair, as a step towards the hearse; in each and all of these views and situations there is but one conclusion possible: that a man should stop his ears against paralysing terror, and run the race that is set before him with a single mind. No one surely could have recoiled with more heartache and terror from the thought of death than our respected lexicographer; and yet we know how little it affected his conduct, how wisely and boldly he walked, and in what a fresh and lively vein he spoke of life. Already an old man, he ventured on his Highland tour; and his heart, bound with triple brass, did not recoil before twenty-seven individual cups of tea.[18] As courage and intelligence are the two qualities best worth a good man's cultivation, so it is the first part of intelligence to recognise our precarious estate in life, and the first part of courage to be not at all abashed before the fact. A frank and somewhat headlong carriage, not looking too anxiously before, not dallying in maudlin regret over the past, stamps the man who is well armoured for this world.

And not only well armoured for himself, but a good friend and a good citizen to boot. We do not go to cowards for tender dealing; there is nothing so cruel as panic; the man who has least fear for his own carcass, has most time to consider others. That eminent chemist who took his walks abroad in tin shoes, and subsisted wholly upon tepid milk, had all his work cut out for him in considerate dealings with his own digestion. So soon as prudence has begun to grow up in the brain, like a dismal fungus, it finds its first expression in a paralysis of generous acts. The victim begins to shrink spiritually; he develops a fancy for parlours with a regulated temperature, and takes his morality on the principle of tin shoes and tepid milk. The care of one important body or soul becomes so engrossing, that all the noises of the outer world begin to come thin and faint into the parlour with the regulated temperature; and the tin shoes go equably forward over blood and rain. To be overwise is to ossify; and the scruple-monger ends by standing stockstill. Now the man who has his heart on his sleeve, and a good whirling weathercock of a brain, who reckons his life as a thing to be dashingly used and cheerfully hazarded, makes a very different acquaintance of the world, keeps all his pulses going true and fast, and gathers impetus as he runs, until, if he be running towards anything better than wildfire, he may shoot up and become a constellation in the end. Lord look after his health, Lord have a care of his soul, says he; and he has at the key of the position, and swashes through incongruity and peril towards his aim. Death is on all sides of him with pointed batteries, as he is on all sides of all of us; unfortunate surprises gird him round; mim-mouthed friends[19] and relations hold up their hands in quite a little elegiacal synod about his path: and what cares he for all this? Being a true lover of living, a fellow with something pushing and spontaneous in his inside, he must, like any other soldier, in any other stirring, deadly warfare, push on at his best pace until he touch the goal. "A peerage or Westminster Abbey!"[20] cried Nelson in his bright, boyish, heroic manner. These are great incentives; not for any of these, but for the plain satisfaction of living, of being about their business in some sort or other, do the brave, serviceable men of every nation tread down the nettle danger,[21] and pass flyingly over all the stumbling-blocks of prudence. Think of the heroism of Johnson, think of that superb indifference to mortal limitation that set him upon his dictionary, and carried him through triumphantly until the end! Who, if he were wisely considerate of things at large, would ever embark upon any work much more considerable than a halfpenny post card? Who would project a serial novel, after Thackeray and Dickens had each fallen in mid-course?[22] Who would find heart enough to begin to live, if he dallied with the consideration of death?

And, after all, what sorry and pitiful quibbling all this is! To forego all the issues of living in a parlour with a regulated temperature—as if that were not to die a hundred times over, and for ten years at a stretch! As if it were not to die in one's own lifetime, and without even the sad immunities of death! As if it were not to die, and yet be the patient spectators of our own pitiable change! The Permanent Possibility is preserved, but the sensations carefully held at arm's length, as if one kept a photographic plate in a dark chamber. It is better to lose health like a spendthrift than to waste it like a miser. It is better to live and be done with it, than to die daily in the sickroom. By all means begin your folio; even if the doctor does not give you a year, even if he hesitates about a month, make one brave push and see what can be accomplished in a week. It is not only in finished undertakings that we ought to honour useful labour. A spirit goes out of the man who means execution, which outlives the most untimely ending. All who have meant good work with their whole hearts, have done good work,[23] although they may die before they have the time to sign it. Every heart that has beat strong and cheerfully has left a hopeful impulse behind it in the world, and bettered the tradition of mankind. And even if death catch people, like an open pitfall, and in mid-career, laying out vast projects, and planning monstrous foundations, flushed with hope, and their mouths full of boastful language, they should be at once tripped up and silenced: is there not something brave and spirited in such a termination? and does not life go down with a better grace, foaming in full body over a precipice, than miserably straggling to an end in sandy deltas? When the Greeks made their fine saying that those whom the gods love die young,[24] I cannot help believing they had this sort of death also in their eye. For surely, at whatever age it overtake the man, this is to die young. Death has not been suffered to take so much as an illusion from his heart. In the hot-fit of life, a tip-toe on the highest point of being, he passes at a bound on to the other side. The noise of the mallet and chisel is scarcely quenched, the trumpets are hardly done blowing, when, trailing with him clouds of glory,[25] this happy-starred, full-blooded spirit shoots into the spiritual land.

NOTES

This essay, which is commonly (and justly) regarded as Stevenson's masterpiece of literary composition, was first printed in the *Cornhill Magazine* for April 1878, Vol. XXXVII, pp. 432-437. In 1881 it was published in the volume *Virginibus Puerisque*. For the success of this volume, as well as for its author's relations with the editor of the *Cornhill*, see our note to *An Apology for Idlers*. It was this article which was selected for reprinting in separate form by the American Committee of the Robert Louis Stevenson Memorial Fund; to every subscriber of ten dollars or more, was given a copy of this essay, exquisitely printed at the De Vinne Press, 1898. Copies of this edition are now eagerly sought by book-collectors; five of them were taken by the Robert Louis Stevenson Club of Yale College, consisting of a few undergraduates of the class of 1898, who subscribed fifty dollars to the fund.

Stevenson's cheerful optimism was constantly shadowed by the thought of Death, and in *Aes Triplex* he gives free rein to his fancies on this universal theme.

[Note 1: The title, *AEs Triplex*, is taken from Horace, *aes triplex circa pectus*, "breast enclosed by triple brass," "aes" used by Horace as a "symbol of indomitable courage."—Lewis's Latin Dictionary.]

[Note 2: *Thug*. This word, which sounds to-day so slangy, really comes from the Hindoos (Hindustani *thaaa*, deceive). It is the name of a religious order in India, ostensibly devoted to the worship of a goddess, but really given to murder for the sake of booty. The Englishmen in India called them *Thugs*, hence the name in its modern general sense.]

[Note 3: *Pyramids ... dule trees*. For pyramids, see our note 25 of chapter II above... *Dule trees*. More properly spelled "dool." A dool was a stake or post used to mark boundaries.]

[Note 4: *The trumpets might sound*. "For if the trumpet give an uncertain sound, who shall prepare himself to the battle?" I *Cor.* XIV, 8.]

[Note 5: *The blue-peter might-fly at the truck*. The blue-peter is a term used in the British navy and widely elsewhere; it is a blue flag with a white square employed often as a signal for sailing. The word is corrupted from *Blue Repeater*, a signal flag. *Truck* is a very small platform at the top of a mast.]

[Note 6: *Balaclava*. A little port near Sebastopol, in the Crimea. During the Crimean War, on the 25 October 1854, occurred the cavalry charge of some six hundred Englishmen, celebrated by Tennyson's universally known poem, *The Charge of the Light Brigade*. It has recently been asserted that the number reported as actually killed in this headlong charge referred to the horses, not to the men.]

[Note 7: *Curtius*. Referring to the story of the Roman youth, Metius Curtius, who in 362 B.C. leaped into a chasm in the Forum, in order to save his country. The chasm immediately closed over him, and Rome was saved. Although the truth of the story has naturally failed to survive the investigations of historical critics, its moral inspiration has been effective in many historical instances.]

[Note 8: *Party for the Derby*. Derby Day, which is the occasion of the most famous annual running race for horses in the world, takes place in the south of England during the week preceding Whitsunday. The race was founded by the Earl of Derby in 1780. It is now one of the greatest holidays in England, and the whole city of London turns out for the event. It is a great spectacle to see the crowd going from London and returning. The most faithful description of the event, the crowds, and the interest excited, may be found in George Moore's novel, *Esther Waters* (1894).]

[Note 9: *The deified Caligula*. Caius Caligula was Roman Emperor from 37 to 41 A. D. He was brought up among the soldiers, who gave him the name Caligula, because he wore the soldier's leather shoe, or half-boot, (Latin *caliga*). Caligula was deified, but that did not prevent him from becoming a madman, which seems to be the best way to account for his wanton cruelty and extraordinary caprices.]

[Note 10: *Baiae* was a small town on the Campanian Coast, ten miles from Naples. It was a favorite summer resort of the Roman aristocracy.]

[Note 11: The *Praetorian Guard* was the body-guard of the Roman emperors. The incident Stevenson speaks of may be found in Tacitus.]

[Note 12: *Job ... Walt Whitman*. The book of *Job* is usually regarded as the most poetical work in the Bible, even exceeding *Psalms* and *Isaiah* in its splendid imaginative language and extraordinary figures of speech. For a literary study of it, the student is recommended to Professor Moulton's edition. Omar Khayyam was a Persian poet of mediaeval times, who became known to English readers through the beautiful paraphrase of some of his stanzas by Edward Fitzgerald, in 1859. If any one will take the trouble to compare a literal prose rendering of Omar (as in N.H. Dole's variorum edition) with the version by Fitzgerald, he will speedily see that the power and beauty of the poem is due far more to the skill of "Old Fitz" than to the original. Thomas Carlyle (1795-1881) was perhaps the foremost writer of English prose in the nineteenth century. Although a consummate literary artist, he was even more influential as a moral tonic. His philosophy and that of Omar represent as wide a contrast as could easily be found. Walt Whitman, the strange American poet (1819-1892), whose famous *Leaves of Grass* (1855) excited an uproar in America, and gave the author a much more serious reputation in Europe. Stevenson's interest in him was genuine, but not partisan, and his essay, *The Gospel According to Walt Whitman (The New Quarterly Magazine,* Oct. 1878), is perhaps the most judicious appreciation in the English language of this singular poet. Job, Omar Khayyam, Carlyle and Whitman, taken together, certainly give a curious collection of what the Germans call *Weltanschauungen.*]

[Note 13: *A vapour, or a show, or made out of the same stuff with dreams.* For constant comparisons of life with a vapour or a show, see Quarles's *Emblems* (1635), though these conventional figures may be found thousands of times in general literature. The latter part of the sentence refers to the *Tempest*, Act IV, Scene I.

　　　"We are such stuff

As dreams are made on, and our little life

Is rounded with a sleep."]

[Note 14: *Permanent Possibility of Sensation.* "Matter then, may be defined, a Permanent Possibility of Sensation."—John Stuart Mill, *Examination of Sir William Hamilton's Philosophy*, Vol. I. Chap. XI.]

[Note 15: *Like the Commander's Statue.* In the familiar story of Don Juan, where the audacious rake accepts the Commander's invitation to supper. For treatments of this theme, see Molière's play *Don Juan*, or Mozart's opera *Don Giovanni*; see also Bernard Shaw's paradoxical play, *Man and Superman*.... *We have something else in hand, thank God, and let him knock.* It is possible that Stevenson's words here are an unconscious reminiscence of Colley Cibber's letter to the novelist Richardson. This unabashed old profligate celebrated the Christmas Day of his eightieth year by writing to the apostle of domestic virtue in the following strain: "Though Death has been cooling his heels at my door these three weeks, I have not had time to see him. The daily conversation of my friends has kept me so agreeably alive, that I have not passed my time better a great while. If you have a mind to make one of us, I will order Death to come another day."]

[Note 16: *All the world over, and every hour.* He might truthfully have said, "every second."]

[Note 17: *A mere bag's end, as the French say.* A cul de sac.]

[Note 18: *Our respected lexicographer ... Highland tour ... triple brass ... twenty-seven individual cups of tea.* Dr. Samuel Johnson's Dictionary appeared in 1755. For his horror of death, his fondness for tea, and his Highland tour with Boswell, see the latter's *Life of Johnson*; consult the late Dr. Hill's admirable index in his edition of the *Life*.]

[Note 19: *Mim-mouthed friends.* See J. Wright's *English Dialect Dictionary.* "Mim-mouthed" means "affectedly prim or proper in speech."]

[Note 20: "*A peerage or Westminster Abbey!*" Horatio Nelson
(1758-1805), the most famous admiral in England's naval history,
who won the great battle of Trafalgar and lost his life in the
moment of victory. Nelson was as ambitious as he was brave, and
his cry that Stevenson quotes was characteristic.]

[Note 21: *Tread down the nettle danger.* Hotspur's words in
King Henry IV, Part I, Act II, Sc. 3. "Out of this nettle, danger, we
pluck this flower, safety."]

[Note 22: *After Thackeray and Dickens had each fallen in
mid-course?* Thackeray and Dickens, dying in 1863 and in 1870
respectively, left unfinished *Denis Duval* and *The Mystery of
Edwin Drood.* Stevenson himself left unfinished what would in
all probability have been his unquestioned masterpiece, *Weir of
Hermiston.*]

[Note 23: *All who have meant good work with their whole
hearts, have done good work.* See Browning's inspiring poem, *Rabbi
Ben Ezra*, XXIII, XXIV, XXV:—

"Not on the vulgar mass
Called "work," must sentence pass,
Things done, which took the eye and had the price;
O'er which, from level stand,
The low world laid its hand,
Found straightway to its mind, could value in a trice:
But all, the world's coarse thumb
And finger failed to plumb,
So passed in making up the main account;

82

All instincts immature,

All purposes unsure,

That weighed not as his work, yet swelled the man's amount:

    Thoughts hardly to be packed

Into a narrow act,

Fancies that broke through language and escaped;

    All I could never be,

    All, men ignored in me,

This, I was worth to God, whose wheel the pitcher shaped."]

[Note 24: *Whom the Gods love die young.* "Quem di diligunt adolescens moritur."—Plautus, *Bacchides*, Act IV, Sc. 7.]

[Note 25: *Trailing with him clouds of glory.* This passage, from Wordsworth's *Ode on the Intimations of Immortality* (1807), was a favorite one with Stevenson, and he quotes it several times in various essays.]

IV

TALK AND TALKERS

I

"Sir, we had a good talk."[1]—JOHNSON.

"As we must account[2] for every idle word, so we must for every idle silence."—FRANKLIN.

There can be no fairer ambition than to excel in talk; to be affable, gay, ready, clear and welcome; to have a fact, a thought, or an illustration, pat to every subject; and not only to cheer the flight of time among our intimates, but bear our part in that great international congress, always sitting, where public wrongs are first declared, public errors first corrected, and the course of public opinion shaped, day by day, a little nearer to the right. No measure comes before Parliament but it has been long ago prepared by the grand jury of the talkers; no book is written that has not been largely composed by their assistance. Literature in many of its branches is no other than the shadow of good talk; but the imitation falls far short of the original in life, freedom and effect. There are always two to a talk, giving and taking, comparing experience and according conclusions. Talk is fluid, tentative, continually "in further search and progress;" while written words remain fixed, become idols even to the writer, found wooden dogmatisms, and preserve flies of obvious error in the amber[3] of the truth. Last and chief, while literature, gagged with linsey-woolsey, can only deal with a fraction of the life of man, talk goes fancy free[4] and may call a spade a spade.[5] It cannot, even if it would, become merely aesthetic or merely classical like literature. A jest intervenes, the solemn humbug is dissolved in laughter, and speech runs forth out of the contemporary groove into the open fields of nature, cheery and cheering, like schoolboys out of school. And it is in talk alone that we can learn our period and ourselves. In short, the first duty of a man is to speak; that is his chief business in this world; and talk, which is the harmonious speech of two or more, is by far the most accessible of pleasures. It costs nothing in money; it is all profit; it completes our education, founds and fosters our friendships, and can be enjoyed at any age and in almost any state of health.

The spice of life is battle; the friendliest relations are still a kind of contest; and if we would not forego all that is valuable in our lot, we must continually face some other person, eye to eye, and wrestle a fall whether in love or enmity. It is still by force of body, or power of character or intellect; that we attain to worthy pleasures. Men and women contend for each other in the lists of love, like rival mesmerists; the active and adroit decide their challenges in the sports of the body; and the sedentary sit down to chess or conversation. All sluggish and pacific pleasures are, to the same degree, solitary and selfish; and every durable bond between human beings is founded in or heightened by some element of competition. Now, the relation that has the least root in matter is undoubtedly that airy one of friendship; and hence, I suppose, it is that good talk most commonly arises among friends. Talk is, indeed, both the scene and instrument of friendship. It is in talk alone that the friends can measure strength, and enjoy that amicable counter-assertion of personality which is the gauge of relations and the sport of life.

A good talk is not to be had for the asking. Humours must first be accorded in a kind of overture or prologue; hour, company and circumstance be suited; and then, at a fit juncture, the subject, the quarry of two heated minds, spring up like a deer out of the wood. Not that the talker has any of the hunter's pride, though he has all and more than all his ardour. The genuine artist follows the stream of conversation as an angler follows the windings of a brook, not dallying where he fails to "kill." He trusts implicitly to hazard; and he is rewarded by continual variety, continual pleasure, and those changing prospects of the truth that are the best of education. There is nothing in a subject, so called, that we should regard it as an idol, or follow it beyond the promptings of desire. Indeed, there are few subjects; and so far as they are truly talkable, more than the half of them may be reduced to three: that I am I, that you are you, and that there are other people dimly understood to be not quite the same as either. Wherever talk may range, it still runs half the time on these eternal lines. The theme being set, each plays on himself as on an instrument; asserts and justifies himself; ransacks his brain for instances and opinions, and brings them forth new-minted, to his own surprise and the admiration of his adversary. All natural talk is a festival of ostentation; and by the laws of the game each accepts and fans the vanity of the other. It is from that reason that we venture to lay ourselves so open, that we dare to be so warmly eloquent, and that we swell in each other's eyes to such a vast proportion. For talkers, once launched, begin to overflow the limits of their ordinary selves, tower up to the height of their secret pretensions, and give themselves out for the heroes, brave, pious, musical and wise, that in their most shining moments they aspire to be. So they weave for themselves with words and for a while inhabit a palace of delights, temple at once and theatre, where they fill the round of the world's dignities, and feast with the gods, exulting in Kudos. And when the talk is over, each goes his way, still flushed with vanity and admiration, still trailing clouds of glory;[6] each declines from the height of his ideal orgie, not in a moment, but by slow declension. I remember, in the *entr'acte* of an afternoon performance, coming forth into the sunshine, in a beautiful green, gardened corner of a romantic city; and as I sat and smoked, the music moving in my blood, I seemed to sit there and evaporate *The Flying Dutchman*[7] (for it was that I had been hearing) with a wonderful sense of life, warmth, well-being and pride; and the noises of the city, voices, bells and marching feet, fell together in my ears like a symphonious orchestra. In the same way, the excitement of a good talk lives for a long while after in the blood, the heart still hot within you, the brain still simmering, and the physical earth swimming around you with the colours of the sunset.

Natural talk, like ploughing, should turn up a large surface of life, rather than dig mines into geological strata. Masses of experience, anecdote, incident, cross-lights, quotation, historical instances, the whole flotsam and jetsam of two minds forced in and in upon the matter in hand from every point of the compass, and from every degree of mental elevation and abasement—these are the material with which talk is fortified, the food on which the talkers thrive. Such argument as is proper to the exercise should still be brief and seizing. Talk should proceed by instances; by the apposite, not the expository. It should keep close along the lines of humanity, near the bosoms and businesses of men, at the level where history, fiction and experience intersect and illuminate each other. I am I, and You are You, with all my heart; but conceive how these lean propositions change and brighten when, instead of words, the actual you and I sit cheek by jowl, the spirit housed in the live body, and the very clothes uttering voices to corroborate the story in the face. Not less surprising is the change when we leave off to speak of generalities—the bad, the good, the miser, and all the characters of Theophrastus[8]—and call up other men, by anecdote or instance, in their very trick and feature; or trading on a common knowledge, toss each other famous names, still glowing with the hues of life. Communication is no longer by words, but by the instancing of whole biographies, epics, systems of philosophy, and epochs of history, in bulk. That which is understood excels that which is spoken in quantity and quality alike; ideas thus figured and personified, change hands, as we may say, like coin; and the speakers imply without effort the most obscure and intricate thoughts. Strangers who have a large common ground of reading will, for this reason, come the sooner to the grapple of genuine converse. If they know Othello and Napoleon, Consuelo and Clarissa Harlowe, Vautrin and Steenie Steenson,[9] they can leave generalities and begin at once to speak by figures.

Conduct and art are the two subjects that arise most frequently and that embrace the widest range of facts. A few pleasures bear discussion for their own sake, but only those which are most social or most radically human; and even these can only be discussed among their devotees. A technicality is always welcome to the expert, whether in athletics, art or law; I have heard the best kind of talk on technicalities from such rare and happy persons as both know and love their business. No human being[10] ever spoke of scenery for above two minutes at a time, which makes me suspect we hear too much of it in literature. The weather is regarded as the very nadir and scoff of conversational topics. And yet the weather, the dramatic element in scenery, is far more tractable in language, and far more human both in import and suggestion than the stable features of the landscape. Sailors and shepherds, and the people generally of coast and mountain, talk well of it; and it is often excitingly presented in literature. But the tendency of all living talk draws it back and back into the common focus of humanity. Talk is a creature of the street and market-place, feeding on gossip; and its last resort is still in a discussion on morals. That is the heroic form of gossip; heroic in virtue of its high pretensions; but still gossip, because it turns on personalities. You can keep no men long, nor Scotchmen[11] at all, off moral or theological discussion. These are to all the world what law is to lawyers; they are everybody's technicalities; the medium through which all consider life, and the dialect in which they express their judgments. I knew three young men who walked together daily for some two months in a solemn and beautiful forest and in cloudless summer weather; daily they talked with unabated zest, and yet scarce wandered that whole time beyond two subjects—theology and love.

And perhaps neither a court of love[12] nor an assembly of divines would have granted their premises or welcomed their conclusions.

Conclusions, indeed, are not often reached by talk any more than by private thinking. That is not the profit. The profit is in the exercise, and above all in the experience; for when we reason at large on any subject, we review our state and history in life. From time to time, however, and specially, I think, in talking art, talk becomes effective, conquering like war, widening the boundaries of knowledge like an exploration. A point arises; the question takes a problematical, a baffling, yet a likely air; the talkers begin to feel lively presentiments of some conclusion near at hand; towards this they strive with emulous ardour, each by his own path, and struggling for first utterance; and then one leaps upon the summit of that matter with a shout, and almost at the same moment the other is beside him; and behold they are agreed. Like enough, the progress is illusory, a mere cat's cradle having been wound and unwound out of words. But the sense of joint discovery is none the less giddy and inspiring. And in the life of the talker such triumphs, though imaginary, are neither few nor far apart; they are attained with speed and pleasure, in the hour of mirth; and by the nature of the process, they are always worthily shared.

There is a certain attitude, combative at once and deferential, eager to fight yet most averse to quarrel, which marks out at once the talkable man. It is not eloquence, not fairness, not obstinacy, but a certain proportion of all of these that I love to encounter in my amicable adversaries. They must not be pontiffs holding doctrine, but huntsmen questing after elements of truth. Neither must they be boys to be instructed, but fellow-teachers with whom I may, wrangle and agree on equal terms. We must reach some solution, some shadow of consent; for without that, eager talk becomes a torture. But we do not wish to reach it cheaply, or quickly, or without the tussle and effort wherein pleasure lies.

The very best talker, with me, is one whom I shall call Spring-Heel'd Jack.[13] I say so, because I never knew anyone who mingled so largely the possible ingredients of converse. In the Spanish proverb, the fourth man necessary to compound a salad, is a madman to mix it: Jack is that madman. I know not what is more remarkable; the insane lucidity of his conclusions, the humorous eloquence of his language, or his power of method, bringing the whole of life into the focus of the subject treated, mixing the conversational salad like a drunken god. He doubles like the serpent, changes and flashes like the shaken kaleidoscope, transmigrates bodily into the views of others, and so, in the twinkling of an eye and with a heady rapture, turns questions inside out and flings them empty before you on the ground, like a triumphant conjuror. It is my common practice when a piece of conduct puzzles me, to attack it in the presence of Jack with such grossness, such partiality and such wearing iteration, as at length shall spur him up in its defence. In a moment he transmigrates, dons the required character, and with moonstruck philosophy justifies the act in question. I can fancy nothing to compare with the *vim* of these impersonations, the strange scale of language, flying from Shakespeare to Kant, and from Kant to Major Dyngwell[14]—

"As fast as a musician scatters sounds
Out of an instrument—"

the sudden, sweeping generalisations, the absurd irrelevant particularities, the wit, wisdom, folly, humour, eloquence and bathos, each startling in its kind, and yet all luminous in the admired disorder of their combination. A talker of a different calibre, though belonging to the same school, is Burly.[15] Burly is a man of great presence; he commands a larger atmosphere, gives the impression of a grosser mass of character than most men. It has been said of him that his presence could be felt in a room you entered blindfold; and the same, I think, has been said of other powerful constitutions condemned to much physical inaction. There is something boisterous and piratic in Burly's manner of talk which suits well enough with this impression. He will roar you down, he will bury his face in his hands, he will undergo passions of revolt and agony; and meanwhile his attitude of mind is really both conciliatory and receptive; and after Pistol has been out-Pistol'd,[16] and the welkin rung for hours, you begin to perceive a certain subsidence in these spring torrents, points of agreement issue, and you end arm-in-arm, and in a glow of mutual admiration. The outcry only serves to make your final union the more unexpected and precious. Throughout there has been perfect sincerity, perfect intelligence, a desire to hear although not always to listen, and an unaffected eagerness to meet concessions. You have, with Burly, none of the dangers that attend debate with Spring-Heel'd Jack; who may at any moment turn his powers of transmigration on yourself, create for you a view you never held, and then furiously fall on you for holding it. These, at least, are my two favourites, and both are loud, copious intolerant talkers. This argues that I myself am in the same category; for if we love talking at all, we love a bright, fierce adversary, who will hold his ground, foot by foot, in much our own manner, sell his attention dearly, and give us our full measure of the dust and exertion of battle. Both these men can be beat from a position, but it takes six hours to do it; a high and hard adventure, worth attempting. With both you can pass days in an enchanted country of the mind, with people, scenery and manners of its own; live a life apart, more arduous, active and glowing than any real existence; and come forth again when the talk is over, as out of a theatre or a dream, to find the east wind still blowing and the chimney-pots of the old battered city still around you. Jack has the far finer mind, Burly the far more honest; Jack gives us the animated poetry, Burly the romantic prose, of similar themes; the one glances high like a meteor and makes a light in darkness; the other, with many changing hues of fire, burns at the sea-level, like a conflagration; but both have the same humour and artistic interests, the same unquenched ardour in pursuit, the same gusts of talk and thunderclaps of contradiction.

Cockshot[17] is a different article, but vastly entertaining, and has been meat and drink to me for many a long evening. His manner is dry, brisk and pertinacious, and the choice of words not much. The point about him is his extraordinary readiness and spirit. You can propound nothing but he has either a theory about it ready-made, or will have one instantly on the stocks, and proceed to lay its timbers and launch it in your presence. "Let me see," he will say. "Give me a moment. I *should* have some theory for that." A blither spectacle than the vigour with which he sets about the task, it were hard to fancy. He is possessed by a demoniac energy, welding the elements for his life, and bending ideas, as an athlete bends a horseshoe, with a visible and lively effort. He has, in theorising, a compass, an art;

what I would call the synthetic gusto; something of a Herbert Spencer,[18] who should see the fun of the thing. You are not bound, and no more is he, to place your faith in these brand-new opinions. But some of them are right enough, durable even for life; and the poorest serve for a cock-shy—as when idle people, after picnics, float a bottle on a pond and have an hour's diversion ere it sinks. Whichever they are, serious opinions or humours of the moment, he still defends his ventures with indefatigable wit and spirit, hitting savagely himself, but taking punishment like a man. He knows and never forgets that people talk, first of all, for the sake of talking; conducts himself in the ring, to use the old slang, like a thorough "glutton,"[19] and honestly enjoys a telling facer from his adversary. Cockshot is bottled effervescency, the sworn foe of sleep. Three-in-the-morning Cockshot, says a victim. His talk is like the driest of all imaginable dry champagnes. Sleight of hand and inimitable quickness are the qualities by which he lives. Athelred,[20] on the other hand, presents you with the spectacle of a sincere and somewhat slow nature thinking aloud. He is the most unready man I ever knew to shine in conversation. You may see him sometimes wrestle with a refractory jest for a minute or two together, and perhaps fail to throw it in the end. And there is something singularly engaging, often instructive, in the simplicity with which he thus exposes the process as well as the result, the works as well as the dial of the clock. Withal he has his hours of inspiration. Apt words come to him as if by accident, and, coming from deeper down, they smack the more personally, they have the more of fine old crusted humanity, rich in sediment and humour. There are sayings of his in which he has stamped himself into the very grain of the language; you would think he must have worn the words next his skin and slept with them. Yet it is not as a sayer of particular good things that Athelred is most to be regarded, rather as the stalwart woodman of thought. I have pulled on a light cord often enough, while he has been wielding the broad-axe; and between us, on this unequal division, many a specious fallacy has fallen. I have known him to battle the same question night after night for years, keeping it in the reign of talk, constantly applying it and re-applying it to life with humorous or grave intention, and all the while, never hurrying, nor flagging, nor taking an unfair advantage of the facts. Jack at a given moment, when arising, as it were, from the tripod, can be more radiantly just to those from whom he differs; but then the tenor of his thoughts is even calumnious; while Athelred, slower to forge excuses, is yet slower to condemn, and sits over the welter of the world, vacillating but still judicial, and still faithfully contending with his doubts.

Both the last talkers deal much in points of conduct and religion studied in the "dry light"[21] of prose. Indirectly and as if against his will the same elements from time to time appear in the troubled and poetic talk of Opalstein.[22] His various and exotic knowledge, complete although unready sympathies, and fine, full, discriminative flow of language, fit him out to be the best of talkers; so perhaps he is with some, not *quite* with me—*proxime accessit*,[23] I should say. He sings the praises of the earth and the arts, flowers and jewels, wine and music, in a moonlight, serenading manner, as to the light guitar; even wisdom comes from his tongue like singing; no one is, indeed, more tuneful in the upper notes. But even while he sings the song of the Sirens, he still hearkens to the barking of the Sphinx. Jarring Byronic notes interrupt the flow of his Horatian humours. His mirth has something of the tragedy of the world for its perpetual background; and he feasts like Don Giovanni to a double orchestra, one lightly sounding for the dance, one pealing Beethoven[24] in the distance. He is not truly reconciled either with life or with himself; and this instant war in his members sometimes divides the man's attention. He does not always, perhaps not often, frankly surrender himself in conversation. He brings into the talk other thoughts than those which he expresses; you are conscious that he keeps an eye on something else, that he does not shake off the world, nor quite forget himself. Hence arise occasional disappointments; even an occasional unfairness for his companions, who find themselves one day giving too much, and the next, when they are wary out of season, giving perhaps too little. Purcel[25] is in another class from any I have mentioned. He is no debater, but appears in conversation, as occasion rises, in two distinct characters, one of which I admire and fear, and the other love. In the first, he is radiantly civil and rather silent, sits on a high, courtly hilltop, and from that vantage-ground drops you his remarks like favours. He seems not to share in our sublunary contentions; he wears no sign of interest; when on a sudden there falls in a crystal of wit, so polished that the dull do not perceive it, but so right that the sensitive are silenced. True talk should have more body and blood, should be louder, vainer and more declaratory of the man; the true talker should not hold so steady an advantage over whom he speaks with; and that is one reason out of a score why I prefer my Purcel in his second character, when he unbends into a strain of graceful gossip, singing like the fireside kettle. In these moods he has an elegant homeliness that rings of the true Queen Anne. I know another person[26] who attains, in his moments, to the insolence of a Restoration comedy, speaking, I declare, as Congreve[27] wrote; but that is a sport of nature, and scarce falls under the rubric, for there is none, alas! to give him answer.

One last remark occurs: It is the mark of genuine conversation that the sayings can scarce be quoted with their full effect beyond the circle of common friends. To have their proper weight they should appear in a biography, and with the portrait of the speaker. Good talk is dramatic; it is like an impromptu piece of acting where each should represent himself to the greatest advantage; and that is the best kind of talk where each speaker is most fully and candidly himself, and where, if you were to shift the speeches round from one to another, there would be the greatest loss in significance and perspicuity. It is for this reason that talk depends so wholly on our company. We should like to introduce Falstaff and Mercutio, or Falstaff and Sir Toby; but Falstaff in talk with Cordelia seems even painful. Most of us, by the Protean[28] quality of man, can talk to some degree with all; but the true talk, that strikes out all the slumbering best of us, comes only with the peculiar brethren of our spirits, is founded as deep as love in the constitution of our being, and is a thing to relish with all our energy, while, yet we have it, and to be grateful for forever.

II[29]

In the last paper there was perhaps too much about mere debate; and there was nothing said at all about that kind of talk which is merely luminous and restful, a higher power of silence, the quiet of the evening shared by ruminating friends. There is something, aside from personal preference, to be alleged in support of this omission. Those who are no chimney-cornerers, who rejoice in the social thunderstorm, have a ground in reason for their choice. They get little rest indeed; but restfulness is a quality for cattle; the virtues are all active, life is alert, and it is in repose that men prepare themselves for evil. On the other hand, they are bruised into a knowledge of themselves and others; they have in a high degree the fencer's pleasure in dexterity displayed and proved; what they get they get upon life's terms, paying for it as they go; and once the talk is launched, they are assured of honest dealing from an adversary eager like themselves. The aboriginal man within us, the cave-dweller, still lusty as when he fought tooth and nail for roots and berries, scents this kind of equal battle from afar; it is like his old primaeval days upon the crags, a return to the sincerity of savage life from the comfortable fictions of the civilised. And if it be delightful to the Old Man, it is none the less profitable to his younger brother, the conscientious gentleman. I feel never quite sure of your urbane and smiling coteries; I fear they indulge a man's vanities in silence, suffer him to encroach, encourage him on to be an ass, and send him forth again, not merely contemned for the moment, but radically more contemptible than when he entered. But if I have a flushed, blustering fellow for my opposite, bent on carrying a point, my vanity is sure to have its ears rubbed, once at least, in the course of the debate. He will not spare me when we differ; he will not fear to demonstrate my folly to my face.

For many natures there is not much charm in the still, chambered society, the circle of bland countenances, the digestive silence, the admired remark, the flutter of affectionate approval. They demand more atmosphere and exercise; "a gale upon their spirits," as our pious ancestors would phrase it; to have their wits well breathed in an uproarious Valhalla.[30] And I suspect that the choice, given their character and faults, is one to be defended. The purely wise are silenced by facts; they talk in a clear atmosphere, problems lying around them like a view in nature; if they can be shown to be somewhat in the wrong, they digest the reproof like a thrashing, and make better intellectual blood. They stand corrected by a whisper; a word or a glance reminds them of the great eternal law. But it is not so with all. Others in conversation seek rather contact with their fellow-men than increase of knowledge or clarity of thought. The drama, not the philosophy, of life is the sphere of their intellectual activity. Even when they pursue truth, they desire as much as possible of what we may call human scenery along the road they follow. They dwell in the heart of life; the blood sounding in their ears, their eyes laying hold of what delights them with a brutal avidity that makes them blind to all besides, their interest riveted on people, living, loving, talking, tangible people. To a man of this description, the sphere of argument seems very pale and ghostly. By a strong expression, a perturbed countenance, floods of tears, an insult which his conscience obliges him to swallow, he is brought round to knowledge which no syllogism would have conveyed to him. His own experience is so vivid, he is so superlatively conscious of himself, that if, day after day, he is allowed to hector and hear nothing but approving echoes, he will lose his hold on the soberness of things and take himself in earnest for a god. Talk might be to such an one the very way of moral ruin; the school where he might learn to be at once intolerable and ridiculous.

This character is perhaps commoner than philosophers suppose. And for persons of that stamp to learn much by conversation, they must speak with their superiors, not in intellect, for that is a superiority that must be proved, but in station. If they cannot find a friend to bully them for their good, they must find either an old man, a woman, or some one so far below them in the artificial order of society, that courtesy may be particularly exercised.

The best teachers are the aged. To the old our mouths are always partly closed; we must swallow our obvious retorts and listen. They sit above our heads, on life's raised dais, and appeal at once to our respect and pity. A flavour of the old school, a touch of something different in their manner—which is freer and rounder, if they come of what is called a good family, and often more timid and precise if they are of the middle class—serves, in these days, to accentuate the difference of age and add a distinction to gray hairs. But their superiority is founded more deeply than by outward marks or gestures. They are before us in the march of man; they have more or less solved the irking problem; they have battled through the equinox of life; in good and evil they have held their course; and now, without open shame, they near the crown and harbour. It may be we have been struck with one of fortune's darts; we can scarce be civil, so cruelly is our spirit tossed. Yet long before we were so much as thought upon, the like calamity befell the old man or woman that now, with pleasant humour, rallies us upon our inattention, sitting composed in the holy evening of man's life, in the clear shining after rain. We grow ashamed of our distresses new and hot and coarse, like villainous roadside brandy; we see life in aerial perspective, under the heavens of faith; and out of the worst, in the mere presence of contented elders, look forward and take patience. Fear shrinks before them "like a thing reproved," not the flitting and ineffectual fear of death, but the instant, dwelling terror of the responsibilities and revenges of life. Their speech, indeed, is timid; they report lions in the path; they counsel a meticulous[31] footing; but their serene, marred faces are more eloquent and tell another story. Where they have gone, we will go also, not very greatly fearing; what they have endured unbroken, we also, God helping us, will make a shift to bear.

Not only is the presence of the aged in itself remedial, but their minds are stored with antidotes, wisdom's simples, plain considerations overlooked by youth. They have matter to communicate, be they never so stupid. Their talk is not merely literature, it is great literature; classic in virtue of the speaker's detachment, studded, like a book of travel, with things we should not otherwise have learnt. In virtue, I have said, of the speaker's detachment—and this is why, of two old men, the one who is not your father speaks to you with the more sensible authority; for in the paternal relation the oldest have lively interests and remain still young. Thus I have known two young men great friends; each swore by the other's father; the father of each swore by the other lad; and yet each pair of parent and child were perpetually by the ears. This is typical: it reads like the germ of some kindly[32] comedy.

The old appear in conversation in two characters: the critically silent and the garrulous anecdotic. The last is perhaps what we look for; it is perhaps the more instructive. An old gentleman, well on in years, sits handsomely and naturally in the bow-window of his age, scanning experience with reverted eye; and chirping and smiling, communicates the accidents and reads the lesson of his long career. Opinions are strengthened, indeed, but they are also weeded out in the course of years. What remains steadily present to the eye of the retired veteran in his hermitage, what still ministers to his content, what still quickens his old honest heart— these are "the real long-lived things"[33] that Whitman tells us to prefer. Where youth agrees with age, not where they differ, wisdom lies; and it is when the young disciple finds his heart to beat in tune with his grey-bearded teacher's that a lesson may be learned. I have known one old gentleman, whom I may name, for he is now gathered to his stock—Robert Hunter, Sheriff of Dumbarton,[34] and author of an excellent law-book still re-edited and republished. Whether he was originally big or little is more than I can guess. When I knew him he was all fallen away and fallen in; crooked and shrunken; buckled into a stiff waistcoat for support; troubled by ailments, which kept him hobbling in and out of the room; one foot gouty; a wig for decency, not for deception, on his head; close shaved, except under his chin—and for that he never failed to apologise, for it went sore against the traditions of his life. You can imagine how he would fare in a novel by Miss Mather;[35] yet this rag of a Chelsea[36] veteran lived to his last year in the plenitude of all that is best in man, brimming with human kindness, and staunch as a Roman soldier under his manifold infirmities. You could not say that he had lost his memory, for he would repeat Shakespeare and Webster and Jeremy Taylor and Burke[37] by the page together; but the parchment was filled up, there was no room for fresh inscriptions, and he was capable of repeating the same anecdote on many successive visits. His voice survived in its full power, and he took a pride in using it. On his last voyage as Commissioner of Lighthouses, he hailed a ship at sea and made himself clearly audible without a speaking trumpet, ruffing the while with a proper vanity in his achievement. He had a habit of eking out his words with interrogative hems, which was puzzling and a little wearisome, suited ill with his appearance, and seemed a survival from some former stage of bodily portliness. Of yore, when he was a great pedestrian and no enemy to good claret, he may have pointed with these minute guns his allocutions to the bench. His humour was perfectly equable, set beyond the reach of fate; gout, rheumatism, stone and gravel might have combined their forces against that frail tabernacle, but when I came round on Sunday evening, he would lay aside Jeremy Taylor's *Life of Christ* and greet me with the same open brow, the same kind formality of manner. His opinions and sympathies dated the man almost to a decade. He had begun life, under his mother's influence, as an admirer of Junius,[38] but on maturer knowledge had transferred his admiration to Burke. He cautioned me, with entire gravity, to be punctilious in writing English; never to forget that I was a Scotchman, that English was a foreign tongue, and that if I attempted the colloquial, I should certainly be shamed: the remark was apposite, I suppose, in the days of David Hume.[39] Scott was too new for him; he had known the author—known him, too, for a Tory; and to the genuine classic a contemporary is always something of a trouble. He had the old, serious love of the play; had even, as he was proud to tell, played a certain part in the history of Shakespearian revivals, for he had successfully pressed on Murray, of the old Edinburgh Theatre, the idea of producing Shakespeare's fairy pieces with great scenic display.[40] A moderate in religion, he was much struck in the last years of his life by a conversation with two young lads, revivalists. "H'm," he would say—"new to me. I have had—h'm—no such experience." It struck him, not with pain, rather with a solemn philosophic interest, that he, a Christian as he hoped, and a Christian of so old a standing, should hear these young fellows talking of his own subject, his own weapons that he had fought the battle of life with,—"and—h'm—not understand." In this wise and grateful attitude he did justice to himself and others, reposed unshaken in his old beliefs, and recognised their limits without anger or alarm. His last recorded remark, on the last night of his life, was after he had been arguing against Calvinism[41] with his minister and was interrupted by an intolerable pang. "After all," he said, "of all the 'isms, I know none so bad as rheumatism." My own last sight of him was some time before, when we dined together at an inn; he had been on circuit, for he stuck to his duties like a chief part of his existence; and I remember it as the only occasion on which he ever soiled his lips with slang—a thing he loathed. We were both Roberts; and as we took our places at table, he addressed me with a twinkle: "We are just what you would call two bob."[42] He offered me port, I remember, as the proper milk of youth; spoke of "twenty-shilling notes"; and throughout the meal was full of old-world pleasantry and quaintness, like an ancient boy on a holiday. But what I recall chiefly was his confession that he had never read *Othello* to an end.[43] Shakespeare was his continual study. He loved nothing better than to display his knowledge and memory by adducing parallel passages from Shakespeare, passages where the same word was employed, or the same idea differently treated. But *Othello* had beaten him. "That noble gentleman and that noble lady—h'm—too painful for me." The same night the boardings were covered with posters, "Burlesque of *Othello*," and the contrast blazed up in my mind like a bonfire. An unforgettable look it gave me into that kind man's soul. His acquaintance was indeed a liberal and pious education.[44] All the humanities were taught in that bare dining-room beside his gouty footstool. He was a piece of good advice; he was himself the instance that pointed and adorned his various talk. Nor could a young man have found elsewhere a place so set apart from envy, fear, discontent, or any of the passions that debase; a life so honest and composed; a soul like an ancient violin, so subdued to harmony, responding to a touch in music—as in that dining-room, with Mr. Hunter chatting at the eleventh hour, under the shadow of eternity, fearless and gentle.

The second class of old people are not anecdotic; they are rather hearers than talkers, listening to the young with an amused and critical attention. To have this sort of intercourse to perfection, I think we must go to old ladies. Women are better hearers than men, to begin with; they learn, I fear in anguish, to bear with the tedious and infantile vanity of the other sex; and we will take more from a woman than even from the oldest man in the way of biting comment. Biting comment is the chief part, whether for profit or amusement, in this business. The old lady that I have in my eye is a very caustic speaker, her tongue, after years of practice, in absolute command, whether for silence or attack. If she chance to dislike you, you will be tempted to curse the malignity of age. But if you chance to please even slightly, you will be listened to with a particular laughing grace of sympathy, and from time to time chastised, as if in play, with a parasol as heavy as a pole-axe. It requires a singular art, as well as the vantage-ground of age, to deal these stunning corrections among the coxcombs of the young. The pill is disguised in sugar of wit; it is administered as a compliment—if you had not pleased, you would not have been censured; it is a personal affair—a hyphen, *a trait d'union*, [45] between you and your censor; age's philandering, for her pleasure and your good. Incontestably the young man feels very much of a fool; but he must be a perfect Malvolio,[46] sick with self-love, if he cannot take an open buffet and still smile. The correction of silence is what kills; when you know you have transgressed, and your friend says nothing and avoids your eye. If a man were made of gutta-percha, his heart would quail at such a moment. But when the word is out, the worst is over; and a fellow with any good-humour at all may pass through a perfect hail of witty criticism, every bare place on his soul hit to the quick with a shrewd missile, and reappear, as if after a dive, tingling with a fine moral reaction, and ready, with a shrinking readiness, one-third loath, for a repetition of the discipline.

There are few women, not well sunned and ripened, and perhaps toughened, who can thus stand apart from a man and say the true thing with a kind of genial cruelty. Still there are some—and I doubt if there be any man who can return the compliment.

The class of men represented by Vernon Whitford in *The Egoist*,[47] says, indeed, the true thing, but he says it stockishly. Vernon is a noble fellow, and makes, by the way, a noble and instructive contrast to Daniel Deronda; his conduct is the conduct of a man of honour; but we agree with him, against our consciences, when he remorsefully considers "its astonishing dryness." He is the best of men, but the best of women manage to combine all that and something more. Their very faults assist them; they are helped even by the falseness of their position in life. They can retire into the fortified camp of the proprieties. They can touch a subject and suppress it. The most adroit employ a somewhat elaborate reserve as a means to be frank, much as they wear gloves when they shake hands. But a man has the full responsibility of his freedom, cannot evade a question, can scarce be silent without rudeness, must answer for his words upon the moment, and is not seldom left face to face with a damning choice, between the more or less dishonourable wriggling of Deronda and the downright woodenness of Vernon Whitford.

But the superiority of women is perpetually menaced; they do not sit throned on infirmities like the old; they are suitors as well as sovereigns; their vanity is engaged, their affections are too apt to follow; and hence much of the talk between the sexes degenerates into something unworthy of the name. The desire to please, to shine with a certain softness of lustre and to draw a fascinating picture of oneself, banishes from conversation all that is sterling and most of what is humorous. As soon as a strong current of mutual admiration begins to flow, the human interest triumphs entirely over the intellectual, and the commerce of words, consciously or not, becomes secondary to the commercing of eyes. But even where this ridiculous danger is avoided, and a man and woman converse equally and honestly, something in their nature or their education falsifies the strain. An instinct prompts them to agree; and where that is impossible, to agree to differ. Should they neglect the warning, at the first suspicion of an argument, they find themselves in different hemispheres. About any point of business or conduct, any actual affair demanding settlement, a woman will speak and listen, hear and answer arguments, not only with natural wisdom, but with candour and logical honesty. But if the subject of debate be something in the air, an abstraction, an excuse for talk, a logical Aunt Sally, then may the male debater instantly abandon hope; he may employ reason, adduce facts, be supple, be smiling, be angry, all shall avail him nothing; what the woman said first, that (unless she has forgotten it) she will repeat at the end. Hence, at the very junctures when a talk between men grows brighter and quicker and begins to promise to bear fruit, talk between the sexes is menaced with dissolution. The point of difference, the point of interest, is evaded by the brilliant woman, under a shower of irrelevant conversational rockets; it is bridged by the discreet woman with a rustle of silk, as she passes smoothly forward to the nearest point of safety. And this sort of prestidigitation, juggling the dangerous topic out of sight until it can be reintroduced with safety in an altered shape, is a piece of tactics among the true drawing-room queens.

The drawing-room is, indeed, an artificial place; it is so by our choice and for our sins. The subjection of women; the ideal imposed upon them from the cradle; and worn, like a hair-shirt, with so much constancy; their motherly, superior tenderness to man's vanity and self-importance; their managing arts—the arts of a civilised slave among good-natured barbarians—are all painful ingredients and all help to falsify relations. It is not till we get clear of that amusing artificial scene that genuine relations are founded, or ideas honestly compared. In the garden, on the road or the hillside, or *tête-à-tête* and apart from interruptions, occasions arise when we may learn much from any single woman; and nowhere more often than in, married life. Marriage is one long conversation, chequered by disputes. The disputes are valueless; they but ingrain the difference; the heroic heart of woman prompting her at once to nail her colours to the mast. But in the intervals, almost unconsciously and with no desire to shine, the whole material of life is turned over and over, ideas are struck out and shared, the two persons more and more adapt their notions one to suit the other, and in process of time, without sound of trumpet, they conduct each, other into new worlds of thought.

NOTES

The two papers on *Talk and Talkers* first appeared in the *Cornhill Magazine*, for April and for August, 1882, Vol. XLV, pp. 410-418, Vol. XLVI, pp. 151-158. The second paper had the title, *Talk and Talkers. (A Sequel.)* For Stevenson's relations with the Editor, see our note to *An Apology for Idlers*. With the publication of the second part, Stevenson's connection with the *Cornhill* ceased, as the magazine in 1883 passed from the hands of Leslie Stephen into those of James Payn. The two papers next appeared in the volume *Memories and Portraits* (1887). The first was composed during the winter of 1881-2 at Davos in the Alps, whither he had gone for his health, the second a few months later.

Writing to Charles Baxter, 22 Feb. 1882, he said, "In an article which will appear sometime in the Cornhill, 'Talk and Talkers,' and where I have full-lengthened the conversation of Bob, Henley, Jenkin, Simpson, Symonds, and Gosse, I have at the end one single word about yourself. It may amuse you to see it." (*Letters*, I, 268.) Writing from Bournemouth, England, in February 1885 to Sidney Colvin, he said, "See how my 'Talk and Talkers' went; every one liked his own portrait, and shrieked about other people's; so it will be with yours. If you are the least true to the essential, the sitter will be pleased; very likely not his friends, and that from various motives." (*Letters*, I, 413.) In a letter to his mother from Davos, dated 9 April 1882, he gives the real names opposite each character in the first paper, and adds, "But pray regard these as secrets."

The art of conversation, like the art of letter-writing, reached its highest point in the eighteenth century; cheap postage destroyed the latter, and the hurly-burly of modern life has been almost too strong for the former. In the French Salons of the eighteenth century, and in the coffeehouses and drawing-rooms of England, good conversation was regarded as a most desirable accomplishment, and was practised by many with extraordinary wit and skill. Swift's satire on *Polite Conversation* (1738) as well as the number of times he discusses the art of conversation in other places, shows how seriously he actually regarded it. Stevenson, like many persons who are forced away from active life, loved a good talk. Good writers are perhaps now more common than good talkers.

FIRST PAPER

115

[Note 1: *Sir, we had a good talk.* This remark was made by the Doctor in 1768, the morning after a memorable meeting at the Crown and Anchor tavern, where he had been engaged in conversation with seven or eight notable literary men. "When I called upon Dr. Johnson next morning," says Boswell, "I found him highly satisfied with his colloquial prowess the preceding evening. 'Well,' said he, 'we had good talk.' BOSWELL: 'Yes, sir, you tossed and gored several persons.'"]

[Note 2: *As we must account.* This remark of Franklin's occurs in *Poor Richard's Almanac* for 1738.]

[Note 3: *Flies … in the amber.* Bartlett gives Martial.]

"The bee enclosed and through the amber shown,

Seems buried in the juice which was his own."

Bacon, Donne, Herrick, Pope and many other authors speak of flies in amber.]

[Note 4: *Fancy free.* See *Midsummer Night's Dream*, Act II, Sc. 2.

"And the imperial votaress passed on,

In maiden meditation, fancy-free."

This has been called the most graceful among all the countless compliments received by Queen Elizabeth. The word "fancy" in the Shaksperian quotation means simply "love."]

[Note 5: *A spade a spade.* The phrase really comes from Aristophanes, and is quoted by Plutarch, as Philip's description of the rudeness of the Macedonians. *Kudos.* Greek word for "pride", used as slang by school-boys in England.]

[Note 6: *Trailing clouds of glory. Trailing with him clouds of glory.* This passage, from Wordsworth's *Ode on the Intimations of Immortality* (1807), was a favorite one with Stevenson, and he quotes it several times in various essays.]

[Note 7: *The Flying Dutchman.* Wagner's *Der Fliegende Holländer* (1843), one of his earliest, shortest, and most beautiful operas. Many German performances are given in the afternoon, and many German theatres have pretty gardens attached, where, during the long intervals (*grosse Pause*) between the acts, one may refresh himself with food, drink, tobacco, and the open air. Germany and German art, however, did not have anything like the influence on Stevenson exerted by the French country, language, and literature.]

[Note 8: *Theophrastus.* A Greek philosopher who died 287-B.C. His most influential work was his *Characters*, which, subsequently translated into many modern languages, produced a whole school of literature known as the "Character Books," of which the best are perhaps Sir Thomas Overbury's *Characters* (1614), John Earle's *Microcosmographie* (1628), and the *Caractères* (1688) of the great French writer, La Bruyère.]

[Note 9: *Consuelo, Clarissa Harlowe, Vautrin, Steenie Steenson. Consuelo* is the title of one of the most notable novels by the famous French authoress, George Sand, (1804-1876), whose real name was Aurore Dupin. *Consuelo* appeared in 1842.... *Clarissa* (1747-8) was the masterpiece of the novelist Samuel Richardson (1689-1761). This great novel, in seven fat volumes, was a warm favorite with Stevenson, as it has been with most English writers from Dr. Johnson to Macaulay. Writing to a friend in December 1877, Stevenson said, "Please, if you have not, and I don't suppose you have, already read it, institute a search in all Melbourne for one of the rarest and certainly one of the best of books—*Clarissa Harlowe*. For any man who takes an interest in the problems of the two sexes, that book is a perfect mine of documents. And it is written, sir, with the pen of an angel." (*Letters*, I, 141.) Editions of *Clarissa* are not so scarce now as they were thirty years ago; several have appeared within the last few years.... *Vautrin* is one of the most remarkable characters in several novels of Balzac; see especially *Pere Goriot* (1834) ... *Steenie Steenson* in Scott's novel *Redgauntlet* (1824).]

[Note 10: *No human being, etc*. Stevenson loved action in novels, and was impatient, as many readers are, when long-drawn descriptions of scenery were introduced. Furthermore, the love for wild scenery has become as fashionable as the love for music; the result being a very general hypocrisy in assumed ecstatic raptures.]

[Note 11: *You can keep no men long, nor Scotchmen at all*. Every Scotchman is a born theologian. Franklin says in his *Autobiography*, "I had caught this by reading my father's books of dispute on Religion. Persons of good sense, I have since observed seldom fall into it, except lawyers, university men, and generally men of all sorts who have been bred at Edinburgh." (Chap. I.)]

[Note 12: *A court of love*. A mediaeval institution of chivalry, where questions of knight-errantry, constancy in love, etc., were discussed and for the time being, decided.]

[Note 13: *Spring-Heel'd Jack*. This is Stevenson's cousin "Bob,"

Robert Alan Mowbray Stevenson (1847-1900), an artist and later

Professor of Fine Arts at University College, Liverpool. He was one of

the best conversationalists in England. Stevenson said of him,

"My cousin Bob, ... is the man likest and most unlike to me that I have ever met.... What was specially his, and genuine, was his faculty for turning over a subject in conversation. There was an insane lucidity in his conclusions; a singular, humorous eloquence in his language, and a power of method, bringing the whole of life into the focus of the subject under hand; none of which I have ever heard equalled or even approached by any other talker." (Balfour's *Life of Stevenson*, I, 103. For further remarks on the cousin, see note to page 104 of the *Life*.)]

[Note 14: *From Shakespeare to Kant, from Kant to Major Dyngwell*. Immanuel Kant, the foremost philosopher of the eighteenth century, born at Königsberg in 1724, died 1804. His greatest work, the *Critique of Pure Reason* (*Kritick der reinen Vernunft*, 1781), produced about the same revolutionary effect on metaphysics as that produced by Copernicus in astronomy, or by Darwin in natural science.... *Major Dyngwell I know not*.]

[Note 15: *Burly*. Burly is Stevenson's friend, the poet William Ernest Henley, who died in 1903. His sonnet on our author may be found in the introduction to this book. Leslie Stephen introduced the two men on 13 Feb. 1875, when Henley was in the hospital, and a very close and intimate friendship began. Henley's personality was exceedingly robust, in contrast with his health, and in his writings and talk he delighted in shocking people. His philosophy of life is seen clearly in his most characteristic poem:

"Out of the night that covers me,
Black as the Pit from pole to pole,
I thank whatever Gods may be
For my unconquerable soul.

In the fell clutch of circumstance
I have not winced nor cried aloud.
Under the bludgeonings of chance
My head is bloody, but unbowed.

Beyond this place of wrath and tears
Looms but the Horror of the shade,
And yet the menace of the years
Finds, and shall find, me unafraid.

It matters not how strait the gate,
How charged with punishments the scroll,
I am the master of my fate:
I am the Captain of my soul."

After the publication of Balfour's *Life of Stevenson* (1901), Mr. Henley contributed to the *Pall Mall Magazine* in December of that year an article called *R.L.S.*, which made a tremendous sensation. It was regarded by many of Stevenson's friends as a wanton assault on his private character. Whether justified or not, it certainly damaged Henley more than the dead author. For further accounts of the relations between the two men, see index to Balfour's *Life*, under the title *Henley*.]

[Note 16: *Pistol has been out-Pistol'd*. The burlesque character in Shakspere's *King Henry IV* and *V*.]

[Note 17: *Cockshot*. (The Late Fleeming Jenkin.) As the note says, this was Professor Fleeming Jenkin, who died 12 June 1885. He exercised a great influence over the younger man. Stevenson paid the debt of gratitude he owed him by writing the *Memoir of Fleeming Jenkin*, published first in America by Charles Scribner's Sons, in 1887.]

[Note 18: *Synthetic gusto; something of a Herbert Spencer*. The English philosopher, Herbert Spencer (1820-1903), whose many volumes in various fields of science and metaphysics were called by their author the *Synthetic Philosophy*. His most popular book is *First Principles* (1862), which has exercised an enormous influence in the direction of agnosticism. His *Autobiography*, two big volumes, was published in 1904, and fell rather flat.]

[Note 19: *Like a thorough "glutton."* This is still the slang of the prize-ring. When a man is able to stand a great deal of punching without losing consciousness or courage, he is called a "glutton for punishment."]

[Note 20: *Athelred*. Sir Walter Simpson, who was Stevenson's companion on the *Inland Voyage*. For a good account of him, see Balfour's *Life of Stevenson*, I, 106.]

[Note 21: *"Dry light."* "The more perfect soul," says Heraclitus, "is a dry light, which flies out of the body as lightning breaks from a cloud." Plutarch, *Life of Romulus.*]

[Note 22: *Opalstein.* This was the writer and art critic, John Addington Symonds (1840-1893). Like Stevenson, he was afflicted with lung trouble, and spent much of his time at Davos, Switzerland, where a good part of his literary work was done. "The great feature of the place for Stevenson was the presence of John Addington Symonds, who, having come there three years before on his way to Egypt, had taken up his abode in Davos, and was now building himself a house. To him the newcomer bore a letter of introduction from Mr. Gosse. On November 5th (1880) Louis wrote to his mother: 'We got to Davos last evening; and I feel sure we shall like it greatly. I saw Symonds this morning, and already like him; it is such sport to have a literary man around.... Symonds is like a Tait to me; eternal interest in the same topics, eternal cross-causewaying of special knowledge. That makes hours to fly.' And a little later he wrote: 'Beyond its splendid climate, Davos has but one advantage—the neighbourhood of J.A. Symonds. I dare say you know his work, but the man is far more interesting.'" (Balfour's *Life of Stevenson*, I, 214.) When Symonds first read the essay *Talk and Talkers*, he pretended to be angry, and said, "Louis Stevenson, what do you mean by describing me as a moonlight serenader?" (*Life*, I, 233.)]

[Note 23: *Proxime accessit.* "He comes very near to it."]

[Note 24: *Sirens ... Sphinx Byronic ... Horatian ... Don Giovanni ... Beethoven.* The Sirens were the famous women of Greek mythology, who lured mariners to destruction by the overpowering sweetness of their songs. How Ulysses outwitted them is well-known to all readers of the *Odyssey.* One of Tennyson's earlier poems, *The Sea-Fairies*, deals with the same theme, and indeed it has appeared constantly in the literature of the world.... The *Sphinx*, a familiar subject in Egyptian art, had a lion's body, the head of some other animal (sometimes man) and wings. It was a symbolical figure. The most famous example is of course the gigantic Sphinx near the Pyramids in Egypt, which has proved to be an inexhaustible theme for speculation and for poetry.... The theatrically tragic mood of *Byron* is contrasted with the easy-going, somewhat cynical epicureanism of Horace.... *Don Giovanni* (1787) the greatest opera of the great composer Mozart (1756-1791), tells the same story told by Molière and so many others. The French composer, Gounod, said that Mozart's *Don Giovanni* was the greatest musical composition that the world has ever seen.... *Beethoven* (1770-1827) occupies in general estimation about the same place in the history of music that Shakspere fills in the history of literature.]

[Note 25: *Purcel.* This stands for Mr. Edmund Gosse (born 1849), a poet and critic of some note, who writes pleasantly on many topics. Many of Stevenson's letters were addressed to him. The two friends first met in London in 1877, and the impression

made by the novelist on the critic may be seen in Mr. Gosse's book
of essays, *Critical Kitcats* (1896).]

[Note 26: *I know another person.* This is undoubtedly
Stevenson's friend Charles Baxter. See the quotation from a
letter to him in our introductory note to this essay. Compare
what Stevenson elsewhere said of him: "I cannot characterise a
personality so unusual in the little space that I can here afford. I
have never known one of so mingled a strain…. He is the only
man I ever heard of who could give and take in conversation with
the wit and polish of style that we find in Congreve's comedies."
(Balfour's *Life of Stevenson*, I, 105.)]

[Note 27: *Restoration comedy … Congreve.* Restoration
comedy is a general name applied to the plays acted in England
between 1660, the year of the restoration of Charles II to the
throne, and 1700, the year of the death of Dryden. This comedy
is as remarkable for the brilliant wit of its dialogue as for its gross
licentiousness. Perhaps the wittiest dramatist of the whole group
was William Congreve (1670-1729).]

[Note 28: *Falstaff … Mercutio … Sir Toby … Cordelia …
Protean.* Sir John Falstaff, who appears in Shakspere's *King Henry
IV*, and again in the *Merry Wives of Windsor*, is generally regarded
as the greatest comic character in literature…. *Mercutio*, the friend
of Romeo; one of the most marvellous of all Shakspere's gentlemen.
He is the Hotspur of comedy, and his taking off by Tybalt "eclipsed
the gaiety of nations."… *Sir Toby Belch* is the genial character in
Twelfth Night, fond of singing and drinking, but no fool withal.

A conversation between Falstaff, Mercutio, and Sir Toby would have taxed even the resources of a Shakspere, and would have been intolerably excellent.... *Cordelia*, the daughter of King Lear, whose sincerity and tenderness combined make her one of the greatest women in the history of poetry.... *Protean*, something that constantly assumes different forms. In mythology, Proteus was the son of Oceanus and Tethys, whose special power was his faculty for lightning changes.

"Have sight of Proteus rising from the sea."—Wordsworth.]

[Note 29: This sequel was called forth by an excellent article in *The Spectator*, for 1 April 1882, and bore the title, *The Restfulness of Talk*. The opening words of this article were as follows:—"The fine paper on 'Talk,' by 'R.L.S.,' in the *Cornhill* for April, a paper which a century since would, by itself, have made a literary reputation, does not cover the whole field."]

[Note 30: *Valhalla*. In Scandinavian mythology, this was the heaven for the brave who fell in battle. Here they had an eternity of fighting and drinking.]

[Note 31: *Meticulous*. Timid. From the Latin, *meticulosus*.]

[Note 32: *Kindly*. Here used in the old sense of "natural." Compare the Litany, "the kindly fruits of the earth."]

[Note 33: "*The real long-lived things*." For Whitman, see our Note 12 of Chapter III above.]

[Note 34: *Robert Hunter, Sheriff of Dumbarton*. Hunter recognised the genius in Stevenson long before the latter became known to the world, and gave him much friendly encouragement.

Dumbarton is a town about 16 miles north-west of Glasgow, in Scotland. It contains a castle famous in history and in literature.]

[Note 35: *A novel by Miss Mather.* The name should be "Mathers." Helen Mathers (Mrs. Henry Reeves), born in 1853, has written a long series of novels, of which *My Lady Greensleeves, The Sin of Hagar* and *Venus Victrix* are perhaps as well-known as they deserve to be.]

[Note 36: *Chelsea.* Formerly a suburb, now a part of London, to the S.W. It is famous for its literary associations. Swift, Thomas Carlyle, Leigh Hunt, George Eliot, Dante Gabriel Rossetti and many other distinguished writers lived in Chelsea at various times. It contains a great hospital, to which Stevenson seems to refer here.]

[Note 37: *Webster, Jeremy Taylor, Burke.* John Webster was one of the Elizabethan dramatists, who, in felicity of diction, approached more nearly to Shakspere than most of his contemporaries. His greatest play was *The Duchess of Malfi* (acted in 1616). Jeremy Taylor (1613-1667), often called the "Shakspere of Divines," was one of the greatest pulpit orators in English history. His most famous work, still a classic, is *Holy Living and Holy Dying* (1650-1). Edmund Burke (1729-1797) the parliamentary orator and author of the *Sublime and Beautiful* (1756), whose speeches on America are only too familiar to American schoolboys.]

[Note 38: *Junius.* No one knows yet who "Junius" was. In the *Public Advertiser* from 21 Jan. 1769 to 21 Jan. 1772, appeared letters signed by this name, which made a sensation. The identity of the author was a favorite matter for dispute during many years.]

[Note 39: *David Hume*. The great Scotch skeptic and philosopher (1711-1776).]

[Note 40: *Shakespeare's fairy pieces with great scenic display.* So far from this being a novelty to-day, it has become rather nauseating, and there are evidences of a reaction in favour of *hearing* Shakspere on the stage rather than *seeing* him.]

[Note 41: *Calvinism.* If this word does not need a note yet, it certainly will before long. The founder of the theological system Calvinism was John Calvin, born in France in 1509. The chief doctrines are Predestination, the Atonement (by which the blood of Christ appeased the wrath of God toward those persons only who had been previously chosen for salvation—on all others the sacrifice was ineffectual), Original Sin, and the Perseverance of the Saints (once saved, one could not fall from grace). These doctrines remained intact in the creed of Presbyterian churches in America until a year or two ago.]

[Note 42: *Two bob.* A pun, for "bob" is slang for "shilling."]

[Note 43: *Never read Othello to an end.* In *A Gossip on a Novel of Dumas's,* Stevenson confessed that there were four plays of Shakspere he had never been able to read through, though for a different reason: they were *Richard III, Henry VI, Titus Andronicus,* and *All's Well that Ends Well.* It is still an open question as to whether or not Shakspere wrote *Titus.*]

[Note 44: *A liberal and pious education.* It was Sir Richard Steele who made the phrase, in *The Tatler,* No. 49: "to love her (Lady Elizabeth Hastings) was a liberal education."]

[Note 45: *Trait d'union*. The French expression simply means "hyphen": literally, "mark of connection."]

[Note 46: *Malvolio*. The conceited but not wholly contemptible character in *Twelfth Night*.]

[Note 47: *The Egoist*. *The Egoist* (1879) is one of the best-known novels of Mr. George Meredith, born 1828. It had been published only a very short time before Stevenson wrote this essay, so he is commenting on one of the "newest" books. Stevenson's enthusiasm for Meredith knew no bounds, and he regarded the *Egoist* and *Richard Feverel* (1859), as among the masterpieces of English literature. *Daniel Deronda*, the last and by no means the best novel of George Eliot (1820-1880), had appeared in 1876.]

V

A GOSSIP ON ROMANCE

In anything fit to be called by the name of reading, the process itself should be absorbing and voluptuous; we should gloat over a book, be rapt clean out of ourselves, and rise from the perusal, our mind filled with the busiest, kaleidoscopic dance of images, incapable of sleep or of continuous thought. The words, if the book be eloquent, should run thence-forward in our ears like the noise of breakers, and the story, if it be a story, repeat itself in a thousand coloured pictures to the eye. It was for this last pleasure that we read so closely, and loved our books so dearly, in the bright, troubled period of boyhood. Eloquence and thought, character and conversation, were but obstacles to brush aside as we dug blithely after a certain sort of incident, like a pig for truffles.[1] For my part, I liked a story to begin with an old wayside inn where, "towards the close of the year 17—," several gentlemen in three-cocked hats were playing bowls. A friend of mine preferred the Malabar coast[2] in a storm, with a ship beating to windward, and a scowling fellow of Herculean proportions striding along the beach; he, to be sure, was a pirate. This was further afield than my home-keeping fancy loved to travel, and designed altogether for a larger canvas than the tales that I affected. Give me a highwayman and I was full to the brim; a Jacobite[3] would do, but the highwayman was my favourite dish. I can still hear that merry clatter of the hoofs along the moonlit lane; night and the coming of day are still related in my mind with the doings of John Rann or Jerry Abershaw;[4] and the words "postchaise," the "great North road,"[5] "ostler," and "nag" still sound in my ears like poetry. One and all, at least, and each with his particular fancy, we read story-books in childhood; not for eloquence or character or thought, but for some quality of the brute incident. That quality was not mere bloodshed or wonder. Although each of these was welcome in its place, the charm for the sake of which we read depended on something different from either. My elders used to read novels aloud; and I can still remember four different passages which I heard, before I was ten, with the same keen and lasting pleasure. One I discovered long afterwards to be the admirable opening of *What will he Do with It?*[6] It was no wonder I was pleased with that. The other three still remain unidentified. One is a little vague; it was about a dark, tall house at night, and people groping on the stairs by the light that escaped from the open door of a sickroom. In another, a lover left a ball, and went walking in a cool, dewy park, whence he could watch the lighted windows and the figures of the dancers as they moved. This was the most sentimental impression I think I had yet received, for a child is somewhat deaf to the sentimental. In the last, a poet, who had been tragically wrangling with his wife, walked forth on the sea-beach on a tempestuous night and witnessed the horrors of a wreck.[7] Different as they are, all these early favourites have a common note—they have all a touch of the romantic.

Drama is the poetry of conduct, romance the poetry of circumstance. The pleasure that we take in life is of two sorts—the active and the passive. Now we are conscious of a great command over our destiny; anon we are lifted up by circumstance, as by a breaking wave, and dashed we know not how into the future. Now we are pleased by our conduct, anon merely pleased by our surroundings. It would be hard to say which of these modes of satisfaction is the more effective, but the latter is surely the more constant. Conduct is three parts of life,[8] they say; but I think they put it high. There is a vast deal in life and letters both which is not immoral, but simply a-moral; which either does not regard the human will at all, or deals with it in obvious and healthy relations; where the interest turns, not upon what a man shall choose to do, but on how he manages to do it; not on the passionate slips and hesitations of the conscience, but on the problems of the body and of the practical intelligence, in clean, open-air adventure, the shock of arms or the diplomacy of life. With such material as this it is impossible to build a play, for the serious theatre exists solely on moral grounds, and is a standing proof of the dissemination of the human conscience. But it is possible to build, upon this ground, the most joyous of verses, and the most lively, beautiful and buoyant tales.

One thing in life calls for another; there is a fitness in events and places. The sight of a pleasant arbour[9] puts it in our minds to sit there. One place suggests work, another idleness, a third early rising and long rambles in the dew. The effect of night, of any flowing water, of lighted cities, of the peep of day, of ships, of the open ocean, calls up in the mind an army of anonymous desires and pleasures. Something, we feel, should happen; we know not what, yet we proceed in quest of it. And many of the happiest hours of life fleet by us in this vain attendance on the genius of the place and moment. It is thus that tracts of young fir, and low rocks that reach into deep soundings, particularly torture and delight me. Something must have happened in such places, and perhaps ages back, to members of my race; when I was a child I tried in vain to invent appropriate games for them, as I still try, just as vainly, to fit them with the proper story. Some places speak distinctly. Certain dank gardens cry aloud for a murder; certain old houses demand to be haunted; certain coasts are set apart for ship-wreck. Other spots again seem to abide their destiny, suggestive and impenetrable, "miching mallecho."[10] The inn at Burford Bridge,[11] with its arbours and green garden and silent, eddying river—though it is known already as the place where Keats wrote some of his *Endymion* and Nelson parted from his Emma—still seems to wait the coming of the appropriate legend. Within these ivied walls, behind these old green shutters, some further business smoulders, waiting for its hour. The old Hawes Inn at the Queen's Ferry makes a similar call upon my fancy. There it stands, apart from the town, beside the pier, in a climate of its own, half inland, half marine—in front, the ferry bubbling with the tide and the guard-ship swinging to her anchor; behind, the old garden with the trees. Americans seek it already for the sake of Lovel and Oldbuck, who dined there at the beginning of the *Antiquary*. But you need not tell me—that is not all; there is some story, unrecorded or not yet complete, which must express the meaning of that inn more fully. So it is with names and faces; so it is with incidents that are idle and inconclusive in themselves, and yet seem like the beginning of some quaint romance, which the all-careless author leaves untold. How many of these romances have we not seen determine at their birth; how many people have met us with a look of meaning in their eye, and sunk at once into trivial acquaintances; to how many places have we not drawn near, with express intimations—"here my destiny awaits me"— and we have but dined there and passed on! I have lived both at the Hawes and Burford in a perpetual flutter, on the heels, as it seemed, of some adventure that should justify the place;

but though the feeling had me to bed at night and called me again at morning in one unbroken round of pleasure and suspense, nothing befell me in either worth remark. The man or the hour had not yet come; but some day, I think, a boat shall put off from the Queen's Ferry, fraught with a dear cargo, and some frosty night a horseman, on a tragic errand, rattle with his whip upon the green shutters of the inn at Burford.[12]

Now, this is one of the natural appetites with which any lively literature has to count. The desire for knowledge, I had almost added the desire for meat, is not more deeply seated than this demand for fit and striking incident. The dullest of clowns tells, or tries to tell, himself a story, as the feeblest of children uses invention in his play; and even as the imaginative grown person, joining in the game, at once enriches it with many delightful circumstances, the great creative writer shows us the realisation and the apotheosis of the day-dreams of common men. His stories may be nourished with the realities of life, but their true mark is to satisfy the nameless longings of the reader, and to obey the ideal laws of the day-dream. The right kind of thing should fall out in the right kind of place; the right kind of thing should follow; and not only the characters talk aptly and think naturally, but all the circumstances in a tale answer one to another like notes in music. The threads of a story come from time to time together and make a picture in the web; the characters fall from time to time into some attitude to each other or to nature, which stamps the story home like an illustration. Crusoe[13] recoiling from the footprint, Achilles shouting over against the Trojans, Ulysses bending the great bow, Christian running with his fingers in his ears, these are each culminating moments in the legend, and each has been printed on the mind's eye forever. Other things we may forget; we may forget the words, although they are beautiful; we may forget the author's comment, although perhaps it was ingenious and true; but these epoch-making scenes, which put the last mark of truth upon a story and fill up, at one blow, our capacity for sympathetic pleasure, we so adopt into the very bosom of our mind that neither time nor tide can efface or weaken the impression. This, then, is the plastic part of literature: to embody character, thought, or emotion in some act or attitude that shall be remarkably striking to the mind's eye. This is the highest and hardest thing to do in words; the thing which, once accomplished, equally delights the schoolboy and the sage, and makes, in its own right, the quality of epics. Compared with this, all other purposes in literature, except the purely lyrical or the purely philosophic, are bastard in nature, facile of execution, and feeble in result. It is one thing to write about the inn at Burford, or to describe scenery with the word-painters; it is quite another to seize on the heart of the suggestion and make a country famous with a legend. It is one thing to remark and to dissect, with the most cutting logic, the complications of life, and of the human spirit; it is quite another to give them body and blood in the story of Ajax[14] or of Hamlet. The first is literature, but the second is something besides, for it is likewise art.

English people of the present day[15] are apt, I know not why, to look somewhat down on incident, and reserve their admiration for the clink of teaspoons and the accents of the curate. It is thought clever to write a novel with no story at all, or at least with a very dull one. Reduced even to the lowest terms, a certain interest can be communicated by the art of narrative; a sense of human kinship stirred; and a kind of monotonous fitness, comparable to the words and air of *Sandy's Mull*, preserved among the infinitesimal occurrences recorded. Some people work, in this manner, with even a strong touch. Mr. Trollope's inimitable clergymen naturally arise to the mind in this connection. But even Mr. Trollope[16] does not confine himself to chronicling small beer. Mr. Crawley's collision with the Bishop's wife, Mr. Melnette dallying in the deserted banquet-room, are typical incidents, epically conceived, fitly embodying a crisis. Or again look at Thackeray. If Rawdon Crawley's blow were not delivered, *Vanity Fair* would cease to be a work of art. That scene is the chief ganglion of the tale; and the discharge of energy from Rawdon's fist is the reward and consolation of the reader. The end of *Esmond* is a yet wider excursion from the author's customary fields; the scene at Castlewood is pure Dumas;[17] the great and wily English borrower has here borrowed from the great, unblushing French thief; as usual, he has borrowed admirably well, and the breaking of the sword rounds off the best of all his books with a manly, martial note. But perhaps nothing can more strongly illustrate the necessity for marking incident than to compare the living fame of *Robinson Crusoe* with the discredit of *Clarissa Harlowe*.[18] *Clarissa* is a book of a far more startling import, worked out, on a great canvas, with inimitable courage and unflagging art. It contains wit, character, passion, plot, conversations full of spirit and insight, letters sparkling with unstrained humanity; and if the death of the heroine be somewhat frigid and artificial, the last days of the hero strike the only note of what we now call Byronism,[19] between the Elizabethans and Byron himself. And yet a little story of a ship-wrecked sailor, with not a tenth part of the style nor a thousandth part of the wisdom, exploring none of the arcana of humanity and deprived of the perennial interest of love, goes on from edition to edition, ever young, while *Clarissa* lies upon the shelves unread. A friend of mine, a Welsh blacksmith, was twenty-five years old and could neither read nor write, when he heard a chapter of *Robinson* read aloud in a farm kitchen. Up to that moment he had sat content, huddled in his ignorance, but he left that farm another man. There were day-dreams, it appeared, divine day-dreams, written and printed and bound, and to be bought for money and enjoyed at pleasure. Down he sat that day, painfully learned to read Welsh, and returned to borrow the book. It had been lost, nor could he find another copy but one that was in English. Down he sat once more, learned English, and at length, and with entire delight, read *Robinson*. It is like the story of a love-chase. If he had heard a letter from *Clarissa*, would he have been fired with the same chivalrous ardour? I wonder. Yet *Clarissa* has every quality that can be shown in prose, one alone excepted—pictorial or picture-making romance. While *Robinson* depends, for the most part and with the overwhelming majority of its readers, on the charm of circumstance.

In the highest achievements of the art of words, the dramatic and the pictorial, the moral and romantic interest, rise and fall together by a common and organic law. Situation is animated with passion, passion clothed upon with situation. Neither exists for itself, but each inheres indissolubly with the other. This is high art; and not only the highest art possible in words, but the highest art of all, since it combines the greatest mass and diversity of the elements of truth and pleasure. Such are epics, and the few prose tales that have the epic weight. But as from a school of works, aping the creative, incident and romance are ruthlessly discarded, so may character and drama be omitted or subordinated to romance. There is one book, for example, more generally loved than Shakespeare, that captivates in childhood, and still delights in age—I mean the *Arabian Nights*—where you shall look in vain for moral or for intellectual interest. No human face or voice greets us among that wooden crowd of kings and genies, sorcerers and beggarmen. Adventure, on the most naked terms, furnishes forth the entertainment and is found enough. Dumas approaches perhaps nearest of any modern to these Arabian authors in the purely material charm of some of his romances. The early part of *Monte Cristo*, down to the finding of the treasure, is a piece of perfect story-telling; the man never breathed who shared these moving incidents without a tremor; and yet Faria is a thing of packthread and Dantès[20] little more than a name. The sequel is one long-drawn error, gloomy, bloody, unnatural and dull; but as for these early chapters, I do not believe there is another volume extant where you can breathe the same unmingled atmosphere of romance. It is very thin and light, to be sure, as on a high mountain; but it is brisk and clear and sunny in proportion. I saw the other day, with envy, an old and a very clever lady setting forth on a second or third voyage into *Monte Cristo*. Here are stories which powerfully affect the reader, which can be reperused at any age, and where the characters are no more than puppets. The bony fist of the showman visibly propels them; their springs are an open secret; their faces are of wood, their bellies filled with bran; and yet we thrillingly partake of their adventures. And the point may be illustrated still further. The last interview between Lucy and Richard Feveril[21] is pure drama; more than that, it is the strongest scene, since Shakespeare, in the English tongue. Their first meeting by the river, on the other hand, is pure romance; it has nothing to do with character; it might happen to any other boy and maiden, and be none the less delightful for the change. And yet I think he would be a bold man who should choose between these passages. Thus, in the same book, we may have two scenes, each capital in its order: in the one, human passion, deep calling unto deep, shall utter its genuine voice; in the second, according circumstances, like instruments in tune, shall build up a trivial but desirable incident, such as we love to prefigure for ourselves; and in the end, in spite of the critics, we may hesitate to give the preference to either. The one may ask more genius—I do not say it does; but at least the other dwells as clearly in the memory.

True romantic art, again, makes a romance of all things. It reaches into the highest abstraction of the ideal; it does not refuse the most pedestrian realism. *Robinson Crusoe* is as realistic as it is romantic:[22] both qualities are pushed to an extreme, and neither suffers. Nor does romance depend upon the material importance of the incidents. To deal with strong and deadly elements, banditti, pirates, war and murder, is to conjure with great names, and, in the event of failure, to double the disgrace. The arrival of Haydn[23] and Consuelo at the Canon's villa is a very trifling incident; yet we may read a dozen boisterous stories from beginning to end, and not receive so fresh and stirring an impression of adventure. It was the scene of Crusoe at the wreck, if I remember rightly, that so bewitched my blacksmith. Nor is the fact surprising. Every single article the castaway recovers from the hulk is "a joy for ever"[24] to the man who reads of them. They are the things that should be found, and the bare enumeration stirs the blood. I found a glimmer of the same interest the other day in a new book, *The Sailor's Sweetheart*,[25] by Mr. Clark Russell. The whole business of the brig *Morning Star* is very rightly felt and spiritedly written; but the clothes, the books and the money satisfy the reader's mind like things to eat. We are dealing here with the old cut-and-dry legitimate interest of treasure trove. But even treasure trove can be made dull. There are few people who have not groaned under the plethora of goods that fell to the lot of the *Swiss Family Robinson*,[26] that dreary family. They found article after article, creature after creature, from milk kine to pieces of ordnance, a whole consignment; but no informing taste had presided over the selection, there was no smack or relish in the invoice; and these riches left the fancy cold. The box of goods in Verne's *Mysterious Island*[27] is another case in point: there was no gusto and no glamour about that; it might have come from a shop. But the two hundred and seventy-eight Australian sovereigns on board the *Morning Star* fell upon me like a surprise that I had expected; whole vistas of secondary stories, besides the one in hand, radiated forth from that discovery, as they radiate from a striking particular in life; and I was made for the moment as happy as a reader has the right to be.

To come at all at the nature of this quality of romance, we must bear in mind the peculiarity of our attitude to any art. No art produces illusion; in the theatre we never forget that we are in the theatre; and while we read a story, we sit wavering between two minds, now merely clapping our hands at the merit of the performance, now condescending to take an active part in fancy with the characters. This last is the triumph of romantic story-telling: when the reader consciously plays at being the hero, the scene is a good scene. Now in character-studies the pleasure that we take is critical; we watch, we approve, we smile at incongruities, we are moved to sudden heats of sympathy with courage, suffering or virtue. But the characters are still themselves, they are not us; the more clearly they are depicted, the more widely do they stand away from us, the more imperiously do they thrust us back into our place as a spectator. I cannot identify myself with Rawdon Crawley or with Eugène de Rastignac,[28] for I have scarce a hope or fear in common with them. It is not character but incident that woos us out of our reserve. Something happens as we desire to have it happen to ourselves; some situation, that we have long dallied with in fancy, is realised in the story with enticing and appropriate details. Then we forget the characters; then we push the hero aside; then we plunge into the tale in our own person and bathe in fresh experience; and then, and then only, do we say we have been reading a romance. It is not only pleasurable things that we imagine in our day-dreams; there are lights in which we are willing to contemplate even the idea of our own death; ways in which it seems as if it would amuse us to be cheated, wounded or calumniated. It is thus possible to construct a story, even of tragic import, in which every incident, detail and trick of circumstance shall be welcome to the reader's thoughts. Fiction is to the grown man what play is to the child; it is there that he changes the atmosphere and tenor of his life; and when the game so chimes with his fancy that he can join in it with all his heart, when it pleases him with every turn, when he loves to recall it and dwells upon its recollection with entire delight, fiction is called romance.

Walter Scott is out and away the king of the romantics. *The Lady of the Lake* has no indisputable claim to be a poem beyond the inherent fitness and desirability of the tale. It is just such a story as a man would make up for himself, walking, in the best health and temper, through just such scenes as it is laid in. Hence it is that a charm dwells undefinable among these slovenly verses, as the unseen cuckoo fills the mountains with his note; hence, even after we have flung the book aside, the scenery and adventures remain present to the mind, a new and green possession, not unworthy of that beautiful name, *The Lady of the Lake*,[29] or that direct, romantic opening,—one of the most spirited and poetical in literature,—"The stag at eve had drunk his fill." The same strength and the same weaknesses adorn and disfigure the novels. In that ill-written, ragged book, *The Pirate*,[30] the figure of Cleveland—cast up by the sea on the resounding foreland of Dunrossness—moving, with the blood on his hands and the Spanish words on his tongue, among the simple islanders—singing a serenade under the window of his Shetland mistress—is conceived in the very highest manner of romantic invention. The words of his song, "Through groves of palm," sung in such a scene and by such a lover, clench, as in a nutshell, the emphatic contrast upon which the tale is built. In *Guy Mannering*,[31] again, every incident is delightful to the imagination; and the scene when Harry Bertram lands at Ellangowan is a model instance of romantic method.

"'I remember the tune well,' he says, 'though I cannot guess what should at present so strongly recall it to my memory.' He took his flageolet from his pocket and played a simple melody. Apparently the tune awoke the corresponding associations of a damsel.... She immediately took up the song—

"'Are these the links of Forth, she said;
   Or are they the crooks of Dee,
Or the bonny woods of Warroch Head
   That I so fain would see?'

"'By heaven!' said Bertram, 'it is the very ballad.'"

On this quotation two remarks fall to be made. First, as
an instance of modern feeling for romance, this famous touch
of the flageolet and the old song is selected by Miss Braddon
for omission. Miss Braddon's idea[32] of a story, like Mrs.
Todgers's idea of a wooden leg,[33] were something strange
to have expounded. As a matter of personal experience,
Meg's appearance to old Mr. Bertram on the road, the ruins
of Derncleugh, the scene of the flageolet, and the Dominie's
recognition of Harry, are the four strong notes that continue
to ring in the mind after the book is laid aside. The second
point is still more curious. The reader will observe a mark
of excision in the passage as quoted by me. Well, here is
how it runs in the original: "a damsel, who, close behind a
fine spring about half-way down the descent, and which had
once supplied the castle with water, was engaged in bleaching
linen." A man who gave in such copy would be discharged
from the staff of a daily paper. Scott has forgotten to prepare
the reader for the presence of the "damsel"; he has forgotten
to mention the spring and its relation to the ruin; and now,

face to face with his omission, instead of trying back and starting fair, crams all this matter, tail foremost, into a single shambling sentence. It is not merely bad English, or bad style; it is abominably bad narrative besides.

Certainly the contrast is remarkable; and it is one that throws a strong light upon the subject of this paper. For here we have a man of the finest creative instinct touching with perfect certainty and charm the romantic junctures of his story; and we find him utterly careless, almost, it would seem, incapable, in the technical matter of style, and not only frequently weak, but frequently wrong in points of drama. In character parts, indeed, and particularly in the Scotch, he was delicate, strong and truthful; but the trite, obliterated features of too many of his heroes have already wearied two generations of readers. At times his characters will speak with something far beyond propriety with a true heroic note; but on the next page they will be wading wearily forward with an ungrammatical and undramatic rigmarole of words. The man who could conceive and write the character of Elspeth of the Craigburnfoot,[34] as Scott has conceived and written it, had not only splendid romantic, but splendid tragic gifts. How comes it, then, that he could so often fob us off with languid, inarticulate twaddle?

It seems to me that the explanation is to be found in the very quality of his surprising merits. As his books are play to the reader, so were, they play to him. He conjured up the romantic with delight, but he had hardly patience to describe it. He was a great day-dreamer, a seer of fit and beautiful and humorous visions, but hardly a great artist; hardly, in the manful sense, an artist at all. He pleased himself, and so he pleases us. Of the pleasures of his art he tasted fully; but of its toils and vigils and distresses never man knew less. A great romantic—an idle child.

NOTES

This essay first appeared in *Longman's Magazine* for November 1882, Vol. I, pp. 69-79. Five years later it was published in the volume *Memories and Portraits* (1887), followed by an article called *A Humble Remonstrance*, which should really be read in connection with this essay, as it is a continuation of the same line of thought. In the eternal conflict between Romanticism and Realism, Stevenson was heart and soul with the former, and fortunately he lived long enough to see the practical effects of his own precepts and influence. When he began to write, Realism in fiction seemed to have absolute control; when he died, a tremendous reaction in favor of the historical romance had already set in, that reached its climax with the death of the century. Stevenson's share in this Romantic revival was greater than that of any other English writer, and as an English review remarked, if it had not been for him most of the new authors would have been Howells and James young men.

This paper was written at Davos in the winter of 1881-2, and in February, writing to Henley, the author said, "I have just finished a paper, 'A Gossip on Romance,' in which I have tried to do, very popularly, about one-half of the matter you wanted me to try. In a way, I have found an answer to the question. But the subject was hardly fit for so chatty a paper, and it is all loose ends. If ever I do my book on the Art of Literature, I shall gather them together and be clear." (*Letters*, I, 269). On Dec. 8, 1884—the same month in which *A Humble Remonstrance* was printed, Stevenson wrote an interesting letter to Henry James, whose views on the art of fiction were naturally contrary to those of his friend. See *Letters*, I, 402.

[Note 1: *Like a pig for truffles*. See the *Epilogue* to Browning's *Pacchiarotto etc.*, Stanza XVIII:—"Your product is—truffles, you hunt with a pig!"]

[Note 2: *The Malabar coast*. A part of India.]

[Note 3: *Jacobite*. After James II was driven from the throne in 1688, his supporters and those of his descendants were called Jacobites. Jacobus is the Latin for James.]

[Note 4: *John Rann or Jerry Abershaw*. John Rann I cannot find. Louis Jeremiah (or Jerry) Abershaw was a highway robber, who infested the roads near London; he was hung in 1795, when scarcely over twenty-one years old.]

[Note 5: *"Great North road."* The road that runs on the east of England up to Edinburgh. Stevenson yielded to the charm that these words had for him, for he began a romance with the title,

The Great North Road, which however, he never finished. It was published as a fragment in *The Illustrated London News*, in 1895.]

[Note 6: *What will he Do with It?* One of Bulwer-Lytton's novels, published in 1858.]

[Note 7: Since traced by many obliging correspondents to the gallery of Charles Kingsley.]

[Note 8: *Conduct is three parts of life*. In *Literature and Dogma* (1873) Matthew Arnold asserted with great emphasis, that conduct was three-fourths of life.]

[Note 9: *The sight of a pleasant arbour*. Possibly a reminiscence of the arbour in *Pilgrim's Progress*, where Christian fell asleep, and lost his roll. "Now about the midway to the top of the hill was a pleasant arbour."]

[Note 10: *"Miching mallecho."* *Hamlet's* description of the meaning of the Dumb Show in the play-scene, Act III, Sc. 2. "Hidden treachery"—see any annotated edition of *Hamlet*.]

[Note 11: *Burford Bridge ... Keats ... Endymion ... Nelson ... Emma ... the old Hawes Inn at the Queen's Ferry*. Burford Bridge is close to Dorking in Surrey, England: in the old inn, Keats wrote a part of his poem *Endymion* (published 1818). The room where he composed is still on exhibition. Two letters by Keats, which are exceedingly important to the student of his art as a poet, were written from Burford Bridge in November 1817. See Colvin's edition of Keats's Letters, pp. 40-46.... "Emma" is Lady Hamilton, whom Admiral Nelson loved.... Queen's Ferry (properly *Queensferry*) is on the Firth of Forth, Scotland. See a few lines below in the text, where Stevenson gives the reference to the opening pages of Scott's novel the *Antiquary*, which begins in the old inn at this place. See also page 105 of the text, and Stevenson's foot note, where he declares that he did make use of Queensferry in his novel *Kidnapped* (1886)(Chapter XXVI).]

[Note 12: Since the above was written I have tried to launch the boat with my own hands in *Kidnapped*. Some day, perhaps, I may try a rattle at the shutters.]

[Note 13: *Crusoe ... Achilles ... Ulysses ... Christian*. When Robinson Crusoe saw the footprint on the sand, and realised he was not alone.... To a reader of to-day the great hero Achilles seems to be all bluster and selfish childishness; the true gentleman of the Iliad is *Hector*.... When Ulysses returned home in the *Odyssey*, he bent with ease the bow that had proved too much for all the suitors of his lonely and faithful wife Penelope.... Christian "had not run far from his own door when his wife and children, perceiving it, began to cry after him to return; but the man put his fingers in his ears and ran on crying, 'Life! Life! eternal Life!'"—*Pilgrim's Progress*.]

[Note 14: *J*. The Greek heavy-weight in Homer's *Iliad*.

[Note 15: *English people of the present day*. This was absolutely true in 1882. But in 1892 a complete revolution in taste had set in, and many of the most hardened realists were forced to write wild romances, or lose their grip on the public. At this time, Stevenson naturally had no idea how powerfully his as yet unwritten romances were to affect the literary market.]

[Note 16: *Mr. Trollope's ... chronicling small beer ... Rawdon Crawley's blow.* Anthony Trollope (1815-1882) wrote an immense number of mildly entertaining novels concerned with the lives and ambitions of English clergymen and their satellites. His best-known book is probably *Barchester Towers* (1857).... *Chronicling small beer* is the "lame and impotent conclusion" with which Iago finishes his poem (*Othello*, Act II, Sc. I).... *Rawdon Crawley's blow* refers to the most memorable scene in Thackeray's great novel, *Vanity Fair* (1847-8), where Rawdon Crawley, the husband of Becky Sharp, strikes Lord Steyne in the face (Chap. LIII). After writing this powerful scene, Thackeray was in a state of tremendous excitement, and slapping his knee, said, "That's Genius!"]

[Note 17: *The end of Esmond ... pure Dumas.* Thackeray's romance *Henry Esmond* (1852) is regarded by many critics as the greatest work of fiction in the English language; Stevenson here calls it "the best of all his books." The scene Stevenson refers to is where Henry is finally cured of his love for Beatrix, and theatrically breaks his sword in the presence of the royal admirer (Book III, Chap. 13). Alexander Dumas (1803-1370), author of *Monte Cristo* and *Les Trois Mousquetaires*. Stevenson playfully calls him "the great, unblushing French thief"; all he means is that Dumas never hesitated to appropriate material wherever he found it, and work it into his romances.]

[Note 18: *The living fame of Robinson Crusoe with the discredit of Clarissa Harlowe.* A strong contrast between the romance of incident

and the analytical novel. For remarks on *Clarissa*, see our Note 9 of Chapter IV above.]

[Note 19: *Byronism*. About the time Lord Byron was publishing *Childe Harold* (1812-1818) a tremendous wave of romantic melancholy swept over all the countries of Europe. Innumerable poems and romances dealing with mysteriously-sad heroes were written in imitation of Byron; and young authors wore low, rolling collars, and tried to look depressed. See Gautier's *Histoire du Romantisme*. Now the death of Lovelace (in a duel) in Richardson's *Clarissa*, was pitched in exactly the Byronic key, though at that time Byron had not been born.... The Elizabethans were of course thoroughly romantic.]

[Note 20: *Faria...Dantès*. Characters in Dumas's *Monte Cristo* (1841-5).]

[Note 21: *Lucy and Richard Feveril*. Usually spelled "Feverel." Stevenson strangely enough, was always a bad speller. The reference here is to one of Stevenson's favorite novels *The Ordeal of Richard Feverel* (1859) by George Meredith. Stevenson's idolatrous praise of this particular scene in the novel is curious, for no greater contrast in English literary style can be found than that between Meredith's and his own. For another reference by Stevenson to the older novelist, see our Note 47 of Chapter IV above.]

[Note 22: *Robinson Crusoe is as realistic as it is romantic*. Therein lies precisely the charm of this book for boyish minds; the details are given with such candour that it seems as if they must all be true. At heart, Defoe was an intense realist, as well as the first English novelist.]

[Note 23: *The arrival of Haydn*. For a note on George Sand's novel *Consuelo* see Note 9 of Chapter IV above.]

[Note 24: *A joy for ever*. The first line of Keats's poem *Endymion* is "A thing of beauty is a joy forever."]

[Note 25: *The Sailor's Sweetheart*. Mr. W. Clark Russell, born in New York in 1844, has written many popular tales of the sea. His first success was *The Wreck of the Grosvenor* (1876); *The Sailor's Sweetheart*, more properly, *A Sailor's Sweetheart*, was published in 1877.]

[Note 26: *Swiss Family Robinson*. A German story, *Der schweizerische Robinson* (1812) by J.D. Wyss (1743-1818). This story is not so popular as it used to be.]

[Note 27: *Verne's Mysterious Island*. Jules Verne, who died at Amiens, France, in 1904, wrote an immense number of romances, which, translated into many languages, have delighted young readers all over the world. *The Mysterious Island* is a sequel to *Twenty Thousand Leagues under the Sea*.]

[Note 28: *Eugène de Rastignac*. A character in Balzac's novel, *Père Goriot*.]

[Note 29: *The Lady of the Lake*. This poem, published in 1810, is as Stevenson implies, not so much a poem as a rattling good story told in rime.]

[Note 30: *The Pirate*. A novel by Scott, published in 1821. It was the cause of Cooper's writing *The Pilot*. See Cooper's preface to the latter novel.]

[Note 31: *Guy Mannering*. Also by Scott. Published 1815.]

[Note 32: *Miss Braddon's idea*. Mary Elizabeth Braddon (Maxwell), born in 1837, published her first novel, *The Trail of the Serpent*, in 1860. She has written a large number of sensational works of fiction, very popular with an uncritical class of readers. Perhaps her best-known book is *Lady Audley's Secret* (1862). It would be well for the student to refer to the scenes in *Guy Mannering* which Stevenson calls the "*Four strong notes*."]

[Note 33: *Mrs. Todgers's idea of a wooden leg*. Mrs. Todgers is a character in Dickens's novel, *Martin Chuzzlewit* (1843-4).]

[Note 34: *Elspeth of the Craigburnfoot*. A character in the *Antiquary* (1816).]

VI

THE CHARACTER OF DOGS

The civilisation, the manners, and the morals of dog-kind[1] are to a great extent subordinated to those of his ancestral master, man. This animal, in many ways so superior, has accepted a position of inferiority, shares the domestic life, and humours the caprices of the tyrant. But the potentate, like the British in India, pays small regard to the character of his willing client, judges him with listless glances, and condemns him in a byword. Listless have been the looks of his admirers, who have exhausted idle terms of praise, and buried the poor soul below exaggerations. And yet more idle and, if possible, more unintelligent has been the attitude of his express detractors; those who are very fond of dogs "but in their proper place"; who say "poo' fellow, poo' fellow," and are themselves far poorer; who whet the knife of the vivisectionist or heat his oven;[2] who are not ashamed to admire "the creature's instinct"; and flying far beyond folly, have dared to resuscitate the theory of animal machines. The "dog's instinct" and the "automaton-dog," in this age of psychology and science, sound like strange anachronisms. An automaton he certainly is; a machine working independently of his control, the heart like the mill-wheel, keeping all in motion, and the consciousness, like a person shut in the mill garret, enjoying the view out of the window and shaken by the thunder of the stones; an automaton in one corner of which a living spirit is confined: an automaton like man. Instinct again he certainly possesses. Inherited aptitudes are his, inherited frailties. Some things he at once views and understands, as though he were awakened from a sleep, as though he came "trailing clouds of glory."[3] But with him, as with man, the field of instinct is limited; its utterances are obscure and occasional; and about the far larger part of life both the dog and his master must conduct their steps by deduction and observation.

The leading distinction[4] between dog and man, after and perhaps before the different duration of their lives, is that the one can speak and that the other cannot. The absence of the power of speech confines the dog in the development of his intellect. It hinders him from many speculations, for words are the beginning of metaphysic. At the same blow it saves him from many superstitions, and his silence has won for him a higher name for virtue than his conduct justifies. The faults of the dog[5] are many. He is vainer than man, singularly greedy of notice, singularly intolerant of ridicule, suspicious like the deaf, jealous to the degree of frenzy, and radically devoid of truth. The day of an intelligent small dog is passed in the manufacture and the laborious communication of falsehood; he lies with his tail, he lies with his eye, he lies with his protesting paw; and when he rattles his dish or scratches at the door his purpose is other than appears. But he has some apology to offer for the vice. Many of the signs which form his dialect have come to bear an arbitrary meaning, clearly understood both by his master and himself; yet when a new want arises he must either invent a new vehicle of meaning or wrest an old one to a different purpose; and this necessity frequently recurring must tend to lessen his idea of the sanctity of symbols. Meanwhile the dog is clear in his own conscience, and draws, with a human nicety, the distinction between formal and essential truth. Of his punning perversions, his legitimate dexterity with symbols, he is even vain; but when he has told and been detected in a lie, there is not a hair upon his body but confesses guilt. To a dog of gentlemanly feeling theft and falsehood are disgraceful vices. The canine, like the human, gentleman demands in his misdemeanours Montaigne's *"je ne sais quoi de genéréux."* [6] He is never more than half ashamed of having barked or bitten; and for those faults into which he has been led by the desire to shine before a lady of his race, he retains, even under physical correction, a share of pride. But to be caught lying, if he understands it, instantly uncurls his fleece.

Just as among dull observers he preserves a name for truth, the dog has been credited with modesty. It is amazing how the use of language blunts the faculties of man——that because vainglory finds no vent in words, creatures supplied with eyes have been unable to detect a fault so gross and obvious. If a small spoiled dog were suddenly to be endowed with speech, he would prate interminably, and still about himself; when we had friends, we should be forced to lock him in a garret; and what with his whining jealousies and his foible for falsehood, in a year's time he would have gone far to weary out our love. I was about to compare him to Sir Willoughby Patterne,[7] but the Patternes have a manlier sense of their own merits; and the parallel, besides, is ready. Hans Christian Andersen,[8] as we behold him in his startling memoirs, thrilling from top to toe with an excruciating vanity, and scouting even along the street for shadows of offence—here was the talking dog.

It is just this rage for consideration that has betrayed the dog into his satellite position as the friend of man. The cat, an animal of franker appetites, preserves his independence. But the dog, with one eye ever on the audience, has been wheedled into slavery, and praised and patted into the renunciation of his nature. Once he ceased hunting[9] and became man's plate-licker, the Rubicon was crossed. Thenceforth he was a gentleman of leisure; and except the few whom we keep working, the whole race grew more and more self-conscious, mannered and affected. The number of things that a small dog does naturally is strangely small. Enjoying better spirits and not crushed under material cares, he is far more theatrical than average man. His whole life, if he be a dog of any pretension to gallantry, is spent in a vain show, and in the hot pursuit of admiration. Take out your puppy for a walk, and you will find the little ball of fur clumsy, stupid, bewildered, but natural. Let but a few months pass, and when you repeat the process you will find nature buried in convention. He will do nothing plainly; but the simplest processes of our material life will all be bent into the forms of an elaborate and mysterious etiquette. Instinct, says the fool, has awakened. But it is not so. Some dogs—some, at the very least—if they be kept separate from others, remain quite natural; and these, when at length they meet with a companion of experience, and have the game explained to them, distinguish themselves by the severity of their devotion to its rules. I wish I were allowed to tell a story which would radiantly illuminate the point; but men, like dogs, have an elaborate and mysterious etiquette. It is their bond of sympathy that both are the children of convention.

The person, man or dog, who has a conscience is eternally condemned to some degree of humbug; the sense of the law in their members[10] fatally precipitates either towards a frozen and affected bearing. And the converse is true; and in the elaborate and conscious manners of the dog, moral opinions and the love of the ideal stand confessed. To follow for ten minutes in the street some swaggering, canine cavalier, is to receive a lesson in dramatic art and the cultured conduct of the body; in every act and gesture you see him true to a refined conception; and the dullest cur, beholding him, pricks up his ear and proceeds to imitate and parody that charming ease. For to be a high-mannered and high-minded gentleman, careless, affable, and gay, is the inborn pretension of the dog. The large dog, so much lazier, so much more weighed upon with matter, so majestic in repose, so beautiful in effort, is born with the dramatic means to wholly represent the part. And it is more pathetic and perhaps more instructive to consider the small dog in his conscientious and imperfect efforts to outdo Sir Philip Sidney.[11] For the ideal of the dog is feudal and religious;[12] the ever-present polytheism, the whip-bearing Olympus of mankind, rules them on the one hand; on the other, their singular difference of size and strength among themselves effectually prevents the appearance of the democratic notion. Or we might more exactly compare their society to the curious spectacle presented by a school—ushers, monitors, and big and little boys—qualified by one circumstance, the introduction of the other sex. In each, we should observe a somewhat similar tension of manner, and somewhat similar points of honour. In each the larger animal keeps a contemptuous good humour; in each the smaller annoys him with wasp-like impudence, certain of practical immunity; in each we shall find a double life producing double characters, and an excursive and noisy heroism combined with a fair amount of practical timidity. I have known dogs, and I have known school heroes that, set aside the fur, could hardly have been told apart; and if we desire to understand the chivalry of old, we must turn to the school playfields or the dungheap where the dogs are trooping.

Woman, with the dog, has been long enfranchised. Incessant massacre of female innocents has changed the proportions of the sexes and perverted their relations. Thus, when we regard the manners of the dog, we see a romantic and monogamous animal, once perhaps as delicate as the cat, at war with impossible conditions. Man has much to answer for; and the part he plays is yet more damnable and parlous[13] than Corin's in the eyes of Touchstone. But his intervention has at least created an imperial situation for the rare surviving ladies. In that society they reign without a rival: conscious queens; and in the only instance of a canine wife-beater that has ever fallen under my notice, the criminal was somewhat excused by the circumstances of his story. He is a little, very alert, well-bred, intelligent Skye, as black as a hat, with a wet bramble for a nose and two cairn-gorms[14] for eyes. To the human observer, he is decidedly well-looking; but to the ladies of his race he seems abhorrent. A thorough elaborate gentleman, of the plume and sword-knot order, he was born with the nice sense of gallantry to women. He took at their hands the most outrageous treatment; I have heard him bleating like a sheep, I have seen him streaming blood, and his ear tattered like a regimental banner; and yet he would scorn to make reprisals. Nay more, when a human lady upraised the contumelious whip against the very dame who had been so cruelly misusing him, my little great-heart gave but one hoarse cry and fell upon the tyrant tooth and nail. This is the tale of a soul's tragedy.[15] After three years of unavailing chivalry, he suddenly, in one hour, threw off the yoke of obligation; had he been Shakespeare he would then have written *Troilus and Cressida*[16] to brand the offending sex; but being only a little dog, he began to bite them. The surprise of the ladies whom he attacked indicated the monstrosity of his offence; but he had fairly beaten off his better angel, fairly committed moral suicide; for almost in the same hour, throwing aside the last rags of decency, he proceeded to attack the aged also. The fact is worth remark, showing as it does, that ethical laws are common both to dogs and men; and that with both a single deliberate violation of the conscience loosens all. "But while the lamp holds on to burn," says the paraphrase, "the greatest sinner may return."[17] I have been cheered to see symptoms of effectual penitence in my sweet ruffian; and by the handling that he accepted uncomplainingly the other day from an indignant fair one, I begin to hope the period of *Sturm und Drang*[18] is closed.

All these little gentlemen are subtle casuists. The duty to the female dog is plain; but where competing duties rise, down they will sit and study them out like Jesuit confessors. [19] I knew another little Skye, somewhat plain in manner and appearance, but a creature compact of amiability and solid wisdom. His family going abroad for a winter, he was received for that period by an uncle in the same city. The winter over, his own family home again, and his own house (of which he was very proud) reopened, he found himself in a dilemma between two conflicting duties of loyalty and gratitude. His old friends were not to be neglected, but it seemed hardly decent to desert the new. This was how he solved the problem. Every morning, as soon as the door was opened, off posted Coolin to his uncle's, visited the children in the nursery, saluted the whole family, and was back at home in time for breakfast and his bit of fish. Nor was this done without a sacrifice on his part, sharply felt; for he had to forego the particular honour and jewel of his day—his morning's walk with my father. And perhaps, from this cause, he gradually wearied of and relaxed the practice, and at length returned entirely to his ancient habits. But the same decision served him in another and more distressing case of divided duty, which happened not long after. He was not at all a kitchen dog, but the cook had nursed him with unusual kindness during the distemper; and though he did not adore her as he adored my father—although (born snob) he was critically conscious of her position as "only a servant"—he still cherished for her a special gratitude. Well, the cook left, and retired some streets away to lodgings of her own; and there was Coolin in precisely the same situation with any young gentleman who has had the inestimable benefit of a faithful nurse. The canine conscience did not solve the problem with a pound of tea at Christmas. No longer content to pay a flying visit, it was the whole forenoon that he dedicated to his solitary friend. And so, day by day, he continued to comfort her solitude until (for some reason which I could never understand and cannot approve) he was kept locked up to break him of the graceful habit. Here, it is not the similarity, it is the difference, that is worthy of remark; the clearly marked degrees of gratitude and the proportional duration of his visits. Anything further removed from instinct it were hard to fancy; and one is even stirred to a certain impatience with a character so destitute of spontaneity, so passionless in justice, and so priggishly obedient to the voice of reason.

There are not many dogs like this good Coolin. and not many people. But the type is one well marked, both in the human and the canine family. Gallantry was not his aim, but a solid and somewhat oppressive respectability. He was a sworn foe to the unusual and the conspicuous, a praiser of the golden mean, a kind of city uncle modified by Cheeryble.[20] And as he was precise and conscientious in all the steps of his own blameless course, he looked for the same precision and an even greater gravity in the bearing of his deity, my father. It was no sinecure to be Coolin's idol; he was exacting like a rigid parent; and at every sign of levity in the man whom he respected, he announced loudly the death of virtue and the proximate fall of the pillars of the earth.

I have called him a snob; but all dogs are so, though in varying degrees. It is hard to follow their snobbery among themselves; for though I think we can perceive distinctions of rank, we cannot grasp what is the criterion. Thus in Edinburgh, in a good part of the town, there were several distinct societies or clubs that met in the morning to—the phrase is technical—to "rake the backets"[21] in a troop. A friend of mine, the master of three dogs, was one day surprised to observe that they had left one club and joined another; but whether it was a rise or a fall, and the result of an invitation or an expulsion, was more than he could guess. And this illustrates pointedly our ignorance of the real life of dogs, their social ambitions and their social hierarchies. At least, in their dealings with men they are not only conscious of sex, but of the difference of station. And that in the most snobbish manner; for the poor man's dog is not offended by the notice of the rich, and keeps all his ugly feeling for those poorer or more ragged than his master. And again, for every station they have an ideal of behaviour, to which the master, under pain of derogation, will do wisely to conform. How often has not a cold glance of an eye informed me that my dog was disappointed; and how much more gladly would he not have taken a beating than to be thus wounded in the seat of piety!

I knew one disrespectable dog. He was far liker a cat; cared little or nothing for men, with whom he merely coexisted as we do with cattle, and was entirely devoted to the art of poaching. A house would not hold him, and to live in a town was what he refused. He led, I believe, a life of troubled but genuine pleasure, and perished beyond all question in a trap. But this was an exception, a marked reversion to the ancestral type; like the hairy human infant. The true dog of the nineteenth century, to judge by the remainder of my fairly large acquaintance, is in love with respectability. A street-dog was once adopted by a lady. While still an Arab, he had done as Arabs do, gambolling in the mud, charging into butchers' stalls, a cat-hunter, a sturdy beggar, a common rogue and vagabond; but with his rise into society he laid aside these inconsistent pleasures. He stole no more, he hunted no more cats; and conscious of his collar he ignored his old companions. Yet the canine upper class was never brought to recognize the upstart, and from that hour, except for human countenance, he was alone. Friendless, shorn of his sports and the habits of a lifetime, he still lived in a glory of happiness, content with his acquired respectability, and with no care but to support it solemnly. Are we to condemn or praise this self-made dog! We praise his human brother. And thus to conquer vicious habits is as rare with dogs as with men. With the more part, for all their scruple-mongering and moral thought, the vices that are born with them remain invincible throughout; and they live all their years, glorying in their virtues, but still the slaves of their defects. Thus the sage Coolin was a thief to the last; among a thousand peccadilloes, a whole goose and a whole cold leg of mutton lay upon his conscience; but Woggs,[22] whose soul's shipwreck in the matter of gallantry I have recounted above, has only twice been known to steal, and has often nobly conquered the temptation. The eighth is his favourite commandment. There is something painfully human in these unequal virtues and mortal frailties of the best. Still more painful is the bearing of those "stammering professors"[23] in the house of sickness and under the terror of death. It is beyond a doubt to me that, somehow or other, the dog connects together, or confounds, the uneasiness of sickness and the consciousness of guilt. To the pains of the body he often adds the tortures of the conscience; and at these times his haggard protestations form, in regard to the human deathbed, a dreadful parody or parallel.

I once supposed that I had found an inverse relation between the double etiquette which dogs obey; and that those who were most addicted to the showy street life among other dogs were less careful in the practice of home virtues for the tyrant man. But the female dog, that mass of carneying[24] affectations, shines equally in either sphere;

rules her rough posse of attendant swains with unwearying tact and gusto; and with her master and mistress pushes the arts of insinuation to their crowning point. The attention of man and the regard of other dogs flatter (it would thus appear) the same sensibility; but perhaps, if we could read the canine heart, they would be found to flatter it in very marked degrees. Dogs live with man as courtiers round a monarch, steeped in the flattery of his notice and enriched with sinecures. To push their favour in this world of pickings and caresses is, perhaps, the business of their lives; and their joys may lie outside. I am in despair at our persistent ignorance. I read in the lives of our companions the same processes of reason, the same antique and fatal conflicts of the right against the wrong, and of unbitted nature with too rigid custom; I see them with our weaknesses, vain, false, inconstant against appetite, and with our one stalk of virtue, devoted to the dream of an ideal; and yet, as they hurry by me on the street with tail in air, or come singly to solicit my regard, I must own the secret purport of their lives is still inscrutable to man. Is man the friend, or is he the patron only? Have they indeed forgotten nature's voice? or are those moments snatched from courtiership when they touch noses with the tinker's mongrel, the brief reward and pleasure of their artificial lives? Doubtless, when man shares with his dog the toils of a profession and the pleasures of an art, as with the shepherd or the poacher, the affection warms and strengthens till it fills the soul. But doubtless, also, the masters are, in many cases, the object of a merely interested cultus, sitting aloft like Louis Quatorze,[25] giving and receiving flattery and favour; and the dogs, like the majority of men, have but forgotten their true existence and become the dupes of their ambition.

NOTES

This article originally appeared in *The English Illustrated Magazine* for May 1883, Vol. I, pp. 300-305. It was accompanied with illustrations by Randolph Caldecott. The essay was later included in the volume *Memories and Portraits* (1887).

The astonishing fidelity and devotion of the dog to his master have certainly been in part repaid by men of letters in all times. A valuable essay might be written on the Dog's Place in Literature; in the poetry of the East, hundreds of years before Christ, the dog's faithfulness was more than once celebrated. One of the most marvellous passages in Homer's *Odyssey* is the recognition of the ragged Ulysses by the noble old dog, who dies of joy. In recent years, since the publication of Dr. John Brown's *Rab and his Friends* (1858), the dog has approached an apotheosis. Among innumerable sketches and stories with canine heroes may be mentioned Bret Harte's extraordinary portrait of *Boonder*: M. Maeterlinck's essay on dogs: Richard Harding Davis's *The Bar Sinister*: Jack London's *The Call of the Wild*: and best of all, Alfred Ollivant's splendid story

Bob, Son of Battle (1898) which has every indication of becoming an English classic. It is a pity that dogs cannot read.

[Note 1: *The morals of dog-kind.* Stevenson discusses this subject again in his essay *Pulvis et Umbra* (1888).]

[Note 2: *Who whet the knife of the vivisectionist or heat his oven.* Stevenson was so sympathetic by nature that once, seeing a man beating a dog, he interfered, crying, "It's not your dog, it's God's dog." On the subject of vivisection, however his biographer says: "It must be laid to the credit of his reason and the firm balance of his judgment that although vivisection was a subject he could not endure even to have mentioned, yet, with all his imagination and sensibility, he never ranged himself among the opponents of this method of inquiry, provided, of course, it was limited, as in England, with the utmost rigour possible."—Balfour's *Life*, II, 217. The two most powerful opponents of vivisection among Stevenson's contemporaries were Ruskin and Browning. The former resigned the Professorship of Poetry at Oxford because vivisection was permitted at the University: and the latter in two poems *Tray* and *Arcades Ambo* treated the vivisectionists with contempt, implying that they were cowards. In Bernard Shaw's clever novel *Cashel Byron's Profession*, The prize-fighter maintains that his profession is more honorable than that of a man who bakes dogs in an oven. This novel, by the way, which he read in the winter of 1887-88, made an extraordinary impression on Stevenson; he recognised its author's originality and cleverness immediately, and was filled with curiosity as to what kind of person this Shaw might be. "Tell me more of the

inimitable author," he cried. It is a pity that Stevenson did not live
to see the vogue of Shaw as a dramatist, for the latter's early novels
produced practically no impression on the public. See Stevenson's
highly entertaining letter to William Archer, *Letters*, II, 107.]

[Note 3: "*Trailing clouds of glory.*" *Trailing with him clouds
of glory.* This passage, from Wordsworth's *Ode on the Intimations
of Immortality* (1807), was a favorite one with Stevenson, and he
quotes it several times in various essays.]

[Note 4: *The leading distinction.* Those who know dogs will
fully agree with Stevenson here.]

[Note 5: *The faults of the dog.* All lovers of dogs will by no
means agree with Stevenson in his enumeration of canine sins.]

[Note 6: *Montaigne's "je ne sais quoi de généreux."* A bit of
generosity. Montaigne's *Essays* (1580) had an enormous influence
on Stevenson, as they have had on nearly all literary men for three
hundred years. See his article in this volume, *Books Which Save
Influenced Me*, and the discussion of the "personal essay" in our
general Introduction.]

[Note 7: *Sir Willoughby Patterne.* Again a character in
Meredith's *Egoist.* See our Note 47 of Chapter IV above.]

[Note 8: *Hans Christian Andersen.* A Danish writer of
prodigious popularity: born 1805, died 1875. His books were
translated into many languages. The "memoirs" Stevenson refers
to, were called *The Story of My Life*, in which the author brought
the narrative only so far as 1847: it was, however, finished by

another hand. He is well known to juvenile readers by his *Stories for Children*.]

[Note 9: *Once he ceased hunting and became man's plate-licker, the Rubicon was crossed*. For a reversion to type, where the plate-licker goes back to hunting, see Mr. London's powerful story, *The Call of the Wild*. ... The "Rubicon" was a small stream separating Cisalpine Gaul from Italy. Caesar crossed it in 49 B. C, thus taking a decisive step in deliberately advancing into Italy. "Plutarch, in his life of Caesar, makes quite a dramatic scene out of the crossing of the Rubicon. Caesar does not even mention it."—B. Perrin's ed. of *Caesar's Civil War*, p. 142.]

[Note 10: *The law in their members. Romans*, VII, 23. "But I see another law in my members."]

[Note 11: *Sir Philip Sidney*. The stainless Knight of Elizabeth's Court, born 1554, died 1586. The pages of history afford no better illustration of the "gentleman and the scholar." Poet, romancer, critic, courtier, soldier, his beautiful life was crowned by a noble death.]

[Note 12: *The ideal of the dog is feudal and religious*. Maeterlinck says the dog is the only being who has found and is absolutely sure of his God.]

[Note 13: *Damnable and parlous than Corin's in the eyes of Touchstone*. See *As You Like It*, Act III, Sc. 2. "Sin is damnation: Thou art in a parlous state, shepherd."]

[Note 14: *Cairn-gorms*. Brown or yellow quartz, found in the mountain of Cairngorm, Scotland, over 4000 feet high. Stevenson's own dog, "Woggs" or "Bogue," was a black Skye terrier, whom the author seems here to have in mind. See Note 20 of this Chapter, below, "Woggs."]

[Note 15: *A Soul's Tragedy.* The title of a tragedy by Browning, published in 1846.]

[Note 16: *Troilus and Cressida.* One of the most bitter and cynical plays ever written; practically never seen on the English stage, it was successfully revived at Berlin, in September 1904.]

[Note 17: "*While the lamp holds on to burn ... the greatest sinner may return.*" From a hymn by Isaac Watts (1674-1748), beginning

"Life is the time to serve the Lord,
The time to insure the great reward;
And while the lamp holds out to burn,
The vilest sinner may return."

Although this stanza has no remarkable merit, many of Watts's hymns are genuine poetry.]

[Note 18: *Sturm und Drang.* This German expression has been well translated "Storm and Stress." It was applied to the literature in Germany (and in Europe) the latter part of the XVIIIth century, which was characterised by emotional excess of all kinds. A typical book of the period was Goethe's *Sorrows of Werther* (*Die Leiden des jungen Werthers,* 1774). The expression is also often applied to the period of adolescence in the life of the individual.]

[Note 19: *Jesuit confessors*. The Jesuits, or Society of Jesus, one
of the most famous religious orders of the Roman Catholic Church,
was founded in 1534 by Ignatius of Loyola and a few others.]

[Note 20: *Modified by Cheeryble*. The Cheeryble Brothers
are characters in Dickens's *Nicholas Nickleby* (1838-9). Dickens
said in his Preface, "Those who take an interest in this tale, will be
glad to learn that the BROTHERS CHEERYBLE live: that their
liberal charity, their singleness of heart, their noble nature ... are no
creations of the Author's brain."]

[Note 21: "*Rake the backets*." The "backet" is a small, square,
wooden trough generally used for ashes and waste.]

[Note 22: *Woggs* (_and Note: Walter, Watty, Woggy, Woggs,
Wog, and lastly Bogue; under which last name he fell in battle some
twelve months ago. Glory was his aim and he attained it; for his
icon, by the hand of Caldecott, now lies among the treasures of the
nation.) Stevenson's well-beloved black Skye terrier. See Balfour's
Life, I, 212, 223. Stevenson was so deeply affected by Woggs's death
that he could not bear ever to own another dog. A Latin inscription
was placed on his tombstone.... This Note was added in 1887,
when the essay appeared in *Memories and Portraits*. "Icon" means
image (cf. *iconoclast*); the word has lately become familiar through
the religious use of icons by the Russians in the war with Japan.
Randolph Caldecott (1846-1886) was a well-known artist and
prominent contributor of sketches to illustrated magazines.]

[Note 23: "*Stammering Professors.*" A "professor" here means simply a professing Christian. Stevenson alludes to the fact that dogs howl fearfully if some one in the house is dying.]

[Note 24: "*Carneying.*" This means coaxing, wheedling.]

[Note 25: *Louis Quatorze.* Louis XIV of France, who died in 1715, after a reign of 72 years, the longest reign of any monarch in history. His absolutism and complete disregard of the people unconsciously prepared the way for the French Revolution in 1789.]

VII

A COLLEGE MAGAZINE

I

All through my boyhood and youth, I was known and pointed out for the pattern of an idler;[1] and yet I was always busy on my own private end, which was to learn to write. I kept always two books in my pocket, one to read, one to write in. As I walked, my mind was busy fitting what I saw with appropriate words; when I sat by the roadside, I would either read, or a pencil and a penny version-book would be in my hand, to note down the features of the scene or commemorate some halting stanzas. Thus I lived with words. And what I thus wrote was for no ulterior use, it was written consciously for practice. It was not so much that I wished to be an author (though I wished that too) as that I had vowed that I would learn to write. That was a proficiency that tempted me; and I practised to acquire it, as men learn to whittle, in a wager with myself. Description was the principal field of my exercise; for to any one with senses there is always something worth describing, and town and country are but one continuous subject. But I worked in other ways also; often accompanied my walks with dramatic dialogues, in which I played many parts; and often exercised myself in writing down conversations from memory.

This was all excellent, no doubt; so were the diaries I sometimes tried to keep, but always and very speedily discarded, finding them a school of posturing[2] and melancholy self-deception. And yet this was not the most efficient part of my training. Good though it was, it only taught me (so far as I have learned them at all) the lower and less intellectual elements of the art, the choice of the essential note and the right word: things that to a happier constitution had perhaps come by nature. And regarded as training, it had one grave defect; for it set me no standard of achievement. So that there was perhaps more profit, as there was certainly more effort, in my secret labours at home. Whenever I read a book or a passage that particularly pleased me, in which a thing was said or an effect rendered with propriety, in which there was either some conspicuous force or some happy distinction in the style, I must sit down at once and set myself to ape that quality. I was unsuccessful, and I knew it; and tried again, and was again unsuccessful and always unsuccessful; but at least in these vain bouts, I got some practice in rhythm, in harmony, in construction and the co-ordination of parts. I have thus played the sedulous ape to Hazlitt, to Lamb, to Wordsworth, to Sir Thomas Browne, to Defoe, to Hawthorne, to Montaigne, to Baudelaire and to Obermann.[3] I remember one of these monkey tricks, which was called *The Vanity of Morals*: it was to have had a second part, *The Vanity of Knowledge*; and as I had neither morality nor scholarship, the names were apt; but the second part was never attempted, and the first part was written (which is my reason for recalling it, ghostlike, from its ashes) no less than three times: first in the manner of Hazlitt, second in the manner of Ruskin,[4] who had cast on me a passing spell, and third, in a laborious pasticcio of Sir Thomas Browne. So with my other works: *Cain*, an epic, was (save the mark!) an imitation of *Sordello: Robin Hood*, a tale in verse, took an eclectic middle course among the fields of Keats, Chaucer and Morris: in *Monmouth*, a tragedy, I reclined on the bosom of Mr. Swinburne; in my innumerable gouty-footed lyrics, I followed many masters; in the first draft of *The King's Pardon*, a tragedy, I was on the trail of no lesser man than John Webster; in the second draft of the same piece, with staggering versatility, I had shifted my allegiance to Congreve, and of course conceived my fable in a less serious vein—for it was not Congreve's verse, it was his exquisite prose, that I admired and sought to copy. Even at the age of thirteen I had tried to do justice to the inhabitants of the famous city of Peebles[5] in the style of the *Book of Snobs*. So I might go on for ever, through all my abortive novels, and down to my later plays,[6] of which I think more tenderly, for they were not only conceived at first under the bracing influence of old Dumas, but have met with, resurrections: one, strangely bettered by another hand, came on the stage itself and was played by bodily actors; the other, originally known as *Semiramis: a Tragedy*, I have observed on bookstalls under the *alias* of *Prince Otto*. But enough has been said to show by what arts of impersonation, and in what purely ventriloquial efforts I first saw my words on paper.

That, like it or not, is the way to learn to write; whether I have profited or not, that is the way. It was so Keats learned,[7] and there was never a finer temperament for literature than Keats's; it was so, if we could trace it out, that all men have learned; and that is why a revival of letters is always accompanied or heralded by a cast back to earlier and fresher models. Perhaps I hear someone cry out: But this is not the way to be original! It is not; nor is there any way but to be born so. Nor yet, if you are born original, is there anything in this training that shall clip the wings of your originality. There can be none more original than Montaigne,[8] neither could any be more unlike Cicero; yet no craftsman can fail to see how much the one must have tried in his time to imitate the other. Burns[9] is the very type of a prime force in letters: he was of all men the most imitative. Shakespeare himself, the imperial, proceeds directly from a school. It is only from a school that we can expect to have good writers; it is almost invariably from a school that great writers, these lawless exceptions, issue. Nor is there anything here that should astonish the considerate. Before he can tell what cadences he truly prefers, the student should have tried all that are possible; before he can choose and preserve a fitting key of words, he should long have practised the literary scales;[10] and it is only after years of such gymnastic that he can sit down at last, legions of words swarming to his call, dozens of turns of phrase simultaneously bidding for his choice, and he himself knowing what he wants to do and (within the narrow limit of a man's ability) able to do it.

And it is the great point of these imitations that there still shines beyond the student's reach his inimitable model. Let him try as he please, he is still sure of failure; and it is a very old and a very true saying that failure is the only highroad to success. I must have had some disposition to learn; for I clear-sightedly condemned my own performances. I liked doing them indeed; but when they were done, I could see they were rubbish. In consequence, I very rarely showed them even to my friends; and such friends as I chose to be my confidants I must have chosen well, for they had the friendliness to be quite plain with me. "Padding," said one. Another wrote: "I cannot understand why you do lyrics so badly." No more could I! Thrice I put myself in the way of a more authoritative rebuff, by sending a paper to a magazine. These were returned; and I was not surprised nor even pained. If they had not been looked at, as (like all amateurs) I suspected was the case, there was no good in repeating the experiment; if they had been looked at—well, then I had not yet learned to write, and I must keep on learning and living. Lastly, I had a piece of good fortune which is the occasion of this paper, and by which I was able to see my literature in print, and to measure experimentally how far I stood from the favour of the public.

II

The Speculative Society is a body of some antiquity, and has counted among its members Scott, Brougham, Jeffrey, Horner, Benjamin Constant, Robert Emmet, and many a legal and local celebrity besides. By an accident, variously explained, it has its rooms in the very buildings of the University of Edinburgh: a hall, Turkey-carpeted, hung with pictures, looking, when lighted up at night with fire and candle, like some goodly dining-room; a passage-like library, walled with books in their wire cages; and a corridor with a fireplace, benches, a table, many prints of famous members, and a mural tablet to the virtues of a former secretary. Here a member can warm himself and loaf and read; here, in defiance of Senatus-consults, he can smoke. The Senatus looks askance at these privileges; looks even with a somewhat vinegar aspect on the whole society; which argues a lack of proportion in the learned mind, for the world, we may be sure, will prize far higher this haunt of dead lions than all the living dogs of the professorate.

I sat one December morning in the library of the Speculative; a very humble-minded youth, though it was a virtue I never had much credit for; yet proud of my privileges as a member of the Spec.; proud of the pipe I was smoking in the teeth of the Senatus; and in particular, proud of being in the next room to three very distinguished students, who were then conversing beside the corridor fire. One of these has now his name on the back of several volumes, and his voice, I learn, is influential in the law courts. Of the death of the second, you have just been reading what I had to say. And the third also has escaped out of that battle of life in which be fought so hard, it may be so unwisely. They were all three, as I have said, notable students; but this was the most conspicuous. Wealthy, handsome, ambitious, adventurous, diplomatic, a reader of Balzac, and of all men that I have known, the most like to one of Balzac's characters, he led a life, and was attended by an ill fortune, that could be properly set forth only in the *Comédie Humaine*. He had then his eye on Parliament; and soon after the time of which I write, he made a showy speech at a political dinner, was cried up to heaven next day in the *Courant*, and the day after was dashed lower than earth with a charge of plagiarism in the *Scotsman*. Report would have it (I daresay, very wrongly) that he was betrayed by one in whom he particularly trusted, and that the author of the charge had learned its truth from his own lips. Thus, at least, he was up one day on a pinnacle, admired and envied by all; and the next, though still but a boy, he was publicly disgraced. The blow would have broken a less finely tempered spirit; and even him I suppose it rendered reckless; for he took flight to London, and there, in a fast club, disposed of the bulk of his considerable patrimony in the space of one winter. For years thereafter he lived I know not how; always well dressed, always in good hotels and good society, always with empty pockets. The charm of his manner may have stood him in good stead; but though my own manners are very agreeable, I have never found in them a source of livelihood; and to explain the miracle of his continued existence, I must fall back upon the theory of the philosopher, that in his case, as in all of the same kind, "there was a suffering relative in the background." From this genteel eclipse he reappeared upon the scene, and presently sought me out in the character of a generous editor. It is in this part that I best remember him; tall, slender, with a not ungraceful stoop; looking quite like a refined gentleman, and quite like an urbane adventurer; smiling with an engaging ambiguity; cocking at you one peaked eyebrow with a great appearance of finesse; speaking low and sweet and thick, with a touch of burr; telling strange tales with singular deliberation and, to a patient listener, excellent effect. After all these ups and downs, he seemed still, like the rich student that he was of yore, to breathe of money; seemed still perfectly sure of himself and certain of his end. Yet he was then upon the brink of his last overthrow. He had set himself to found the strangest thing in our society: one of those periodical sheets from which men suppose themselves to learn opinions; in which young gentlemen from the universities are encouraged, at so much a line, to garble facts, insult foreign nations and calumniate private individuals; and which are now the source of glory, so that if a man's name be often enough printed there, he becomes a kind of demigod; and people will pardon him when he talks back and forth, as they do for Mr. Gladstone; and crowd him to suffocation on railway platforms, as they did the other day to General Boulanger; and buy his literary works, as I hope you have just done for me. Our fathers, when they were upon some great enterprise, would sacrifice a life; building, it may be, a favourite slave into the foundations of their palace. It was with his own life that my companion disarmed the envy of the gods. He fought his paper single-handed; trusting no one, for he was something of a cynic; up early and down late, for he was nothing of a sluggard; daily earwigging influential men, for he was a master of ingratiation. In that slender and silken fellow there must have been a rare vein of courage, that he should thus have died at his employment; and doubtless ambition spoke loudly in his ear, and doubtless love also, for it seems there was a marriage in his view had he succeeded. But he died, and his paper died after him; and of all this grace, and tact, and courage, it must seem to our blind eyes as if there had come literally nothing.

These three students sat, as I was saying, in the corridor, under the mural tablet that records the virtues of Machean, the former secretary. We would often smile at that ineloquent memorial, and thought it a poor thing to come into the world at all and leave no more behind one than Machean. And yet of these three, two are gone and have left less; and this book, perhaps, when it is old and foxy, and some one picks it up in a corner of a book-shop, and glances through it, smiling at the old, graceless turns of speech, and perhaps for the love of *Alma Mater* (which may be still extant and flourishing) buys it, not without haggling, for some pence—this book may alone preserve a memory of James Walter Ferrier and Robert Glasgow Brown.

Their thoughts ran very differently on that December morning; they were all on fire with ambition; and when they had called me in to them, and made me a sharer in their design, I too became drunken with pride and hope. We were to found a University magazine. A pair of little, active brothers—Livingstone by name, great skippers on the foot, great rubbers of the hands, who kept a book-shop over against the University building—had been debauched to play the part of publishers. We four were to be conjunct editors, and, what was the main point of the concern, to print our own works; while, by every rule of arithmetic—

that flatterer of credulity—the adventure must succeed and bring great profit. Well, well: it was a bright vision. I went home that morning walking upon air. To have been chosen by these three distinguished students was to me the most unspeakable advance; it was my first draught of consideration; it reconciled me to myself and to my fellow-men; and as I steered round the railings at the Tron, I could not withhold my lips from smiling publicly. Yet, in the bottom of my heart, I knew that magazine would be a grim fiasco; I knew it would not be worth reading; I knew, even if it were, that nobody would read it; and I kept wondering, how I should be able, upon my compact income of twelve pounds per annum, payable monthly, to meet my share in the expense. It was a comfortable thought to me that I had a father.

The magazine appeared, in a yellow cover which was the best part of it, for at least it was unassuming; it ran four months in undisturbed obscurity, and died without a gasp. The first number was edited by all four of us with prodigious bustle; the second fell principally into the hands of Ferrier and me; the third I edited alone; and it has long been a solemn question who it was that edited the fourth. It would perhaps be still more difficult to say who read it. Poor yellow sheet, that looked so hopefully in the Livingstones' window! Poor, harmless paper, that might have gone to print a *Shakespeare* on, and was instead so clumsily defaced with nonsense! And, shall I say, Poor Editors? I cannot pity myself, to whom it was all pure gain. It was no news to me, but only the wholesome confirmation of my judgment, when the magazine struggled into half-birth, and instantly sickened and subsided into night. I had sent a copy to the lady with whom my heart was at that time somewhat engaged, and who did all that in her lay to break it; and she, with some tact, passed over the gift and my cherished contributions in silence. I will not say that I was pleased at this; but I will tell her now, if by any chance she takes up the work of her former servant, that I thought the better of her taste. I cleared the decks after this lost engagement; had the necessary interview with my father, which passed off not amiss; paid over my share of the expense to the two little, active brothers, who rubbed their hands as much, but methought skipped rather less than formerly, having perhaps, these two also, embarked upon the enterprise with some graceful illusions; and then, reviewing the whole episode, I told myself that the time was not yet ripe, nor the man ready; and to work I went again with my penny version-books, having fallen back in one day from the printed author to the manuscript student.

III

From this defunct periodical I am going to reprint one of my own papers. The poor little piece is all tail-foremost. I have done my best to straighten its array, I have pruned it fearlessly, and it remains invertebrate and wordy. No self-respecting magazine would print the thing; and here you behold it in a bound volume, not for any worth of its own, but for the sake of the man whom it purports dimly to represent and some of whose sayings it preserves; so that in this volume of Memories and Portraits, Robert Young, the Swanston gardener, may stand alongside of John Todd, the Swanston shepherd. Not that John and Robert drew very close together in their lives; for John was rough, he smelt of the windy brae; and Robert was gentle, and smacked of the garden in the hollow. Perhaps it is to my shame that I liked John the better of the two; he had grit and dash, and that salt of the Old Adam that pleases men with any savage inheritance of blood; and he was a wayfarer besides, and took my gipsy fancy. But however that may be, and however Robert's profile may be blurred in the boyish sketch that follows, he was a man of a most quaint and beautiful nature, whom, if it were possible to recast a piece of work so old, I should like well to draw again with a maturer touch. And as I think of him and of John, I wonder in what other country two such men would be found dwelling together, in a hamlet of some twenty cottages, in the woody fold of a green hill.

NOTES

This article made its first appearance in the volume
Memories and Portraits (1887). It was divided into three parts. The

interest of this essay is almost wholly autobiographical, telling
us, with more or less seriousness, how its author "learned to
write." After Stevenson became famous, this confession attracted
universal attention, and is now one of the best-known of all his
compositions. Many youthful aspirants for literary fame have
been moved by its perusal to adopt a similar method; but while
Stevenson's system, if faithfully followed, would doubtless correct
many faults, it would not of itself enable a man to write another *Aes
Triplex* or *Treasure Island*. It was genius, not industry, that placed
Stevenson in English literature.

[Note 1: *Pattern of an Idler*. See his essay in this volume, *An
Apology for Idlers*.]

[Note 2: *A school of posturing*. It is a nice psychological
question whether or not it is possible for one to write a diary with
absolutely no thought of its being read by some one else.]

[Note 3: *Hazlitt, to Lamb, to Wordsworth, to Sir Thomas
Browne, to Defoe, to Hawthorne, to Montaigne, to Beaudelaire, and
to Obermann*. For Hazlitt, see Note 19 of Chapter II above. Charles
Lamb (1775-1834), author of the delightful *Essays of Elia* (1822-
24), the *tone* of which book is often echoed in Stevenson's essays....
Sir Thomas Browne (1605-1682), regarded by many as the greatest
prose writer of the seventeenth century; his best books are *Religio
Medici* (the religion of a physician), 1642, and *Urn Burial* (1658).
The 300th anniversary of his birth was widely celebrated on 19
October 1905.... Daniel Defoe (1661-1731), an enormously
prolific writer; his first important novel, *Robinson Crusoe* (followed

by many others) was written when he was 58 years old.... Nathaniel Hawthorne, the greatest literary artist that America has ever produced was born 4 July 1804, and died in 1864. His best novel (the finest in American Literature) was *The Scarlet Letter* (1850).... Montaigne. Stevenson was heavily indebted to this wonderful genius. See Note 4 of Chapter VI above. ... Charles Baudelaire (1821-1867) wrote the brilliant and decadent *Fleurs du Mai* (1857-61). He translated Poe into French, and was partly responsible for Poe's immense vogue in France. Had Baudelaire's French followers possessed the power of their master, we should be able to forgive them for writing.... Obermann. *Òbermann* is the title of a story by the French writer Etienne Pivert de Sénancour (1770-1846). The book, which appeared in 1804, is full of vague melancholy, in the Werther fashion, and is more of a psychological study than a novel. In recent years, *Amiel's Journal* and Sienkiewicz's *Without Dogma* belong to the same school of literature. Matthew Arnold was fond of quoting from Sénancour's *Obermann*.]

[Note 4: *Ruskin* ... *Pasticcio* ... *Bordello* ... *Morris* ... *Swinburne* ... *John Webster* ... *Congreve*. These names exhibit the astonishing variety of Stevenson's youthful attempts, for they represent nearly every possible style of composition. John Ruskin (1819-1900) exercised a greater influence thirty years ago than he does to-day Stevenson in the words "a passing spell," seems to apologise for having been influenced by him at all.... Pasticcio, an Italian word, meaning "pie": Swinburne uses it in the sense of "medley," which is about the same as its significance here. *Sordello*:

Stevenson naturally accompanies this statement with a parenthetical exclamation. *Sordello*, published in 1840, is the most obscure of all Browning's poems, and for many years blinded critics to the poet's genius. Innumerable are the witticisms aimed at this opaque work. See, for example, W. Sharp's *Life of Browning* ... William Morris (1834-96), author of the *Earthly Paradise* (1868-70): for his position and influence in XIXth century literature see H.A. Beers, *History of English Romanticism*, Vol. II.... Algernon Charles Swinburne, born 1837, generally regarded (1906) as England's foremost living poet, is famous chiefly for the melodies of his verse. His influence seems to be steadily declining and he is certainly not so much read as formerly.... For John Webster and Congreve, see Notes 37 and 26 of Chapter IV above.]

[Note 5: *City of Peebles in the style of the Book of Snobs.* Thackeray's *Book of Snobs* was published in 1848. Peebles is the county town of Peebles County in the South of Scotland.]

[Note 6: *My later plays*, etc. Stevenson's four plays were not successful. They were all written in collaboration with W.E. Henley. *Deacon Brodie* was printed in 1880: *Admiral Guinea* and *Beau Austin* in 1884: *Macaire* in 1885. In 1892, the first three were published in one volume, under the title *Three Plays*: In 1896 all four appeared in a volume called *Four Plays*. At the time the essay *A College Magazine* was published, only one of these plays had been acted, *Deacon Brodie*, to which Stevenson refers in our text. This "came on the stage itself and was played by bodily actors" at Pullan's *Theatre of Varieties*, Bradford, England, 28 December 1882, and in March 1883 at Her Majesty's Theatre, Aberdeen, "when it was styled a 'New Scotch National Drama.'"—Prideaux, *Bibliography*, p. 10. It was later produced at Prince's Theatre, London, 2 July 1884, and in Montreal, 26 September 1887. *Beau Austin* was played at the Haymarket Theatre, London, 3 Nov. 1890. *Admiral Guinea* was played at the *Avenue Theatre*, on the afternoon of 29 Nov. 1897, and, like the others, was not successful. *The Athenaeum* for 4 Dec. 1897 contains an interesting criticism of this drama…. *Semiramis* was the original plan of a "tragedy," which Stevenson afterwards rewrote as a novel, *Prince Otto*, and published in 1885.]

[Note 7: *It was so Keats learned*. This must be swallowed with a grain of salt. The best criticism of the poetry of Keats is contained in his own *Letters*, which have been edited by Colvin and by Forman.]

[Note 8: *Montaigne … Cicero*. Montaigne, as a child, spoke Latin before he could French: see his *Essays*. Montaigne is always original, frank, sincere: Cicero (in his orations) is always a *Poseur*.]

[Note 9: *Burns … Shakespeare*. Some reflection on, and investigation of these statements by Stevenson, will be highly beneficial to the student.]

[Note 10: The literary scales. It is very interesting to note that Thomas Carlyle had completely mastered the technique of ordinary prose composition, before he deliberately began to write in his own picturesque style, which has been called "Carlylese"; note the enormous difference in style between his *Life of Schiller* (1825) and his *Sartor Resartus* (1833-4). Carlyle would be a shining illustration of the point Stevenson is trying to make.]

No notes have been added to the second and third parts of this essay, as these portions are unimportant, and may be omitted by the student; they are really introductory to something quite different, and are printed in our edition only to make this essay complete.

VIII

BOOKS WHICH HAVE INFLUENCED ME[1]

The Editor[2] has somewhat insidiously laid a trap for his correspondents, the question put appearing at first so innocent, truly cutting so deep. It is not, indeed, until after some reconnaissance and review that the writer awakes to find himself engaged upon something in the nature of autobiography, or, perhaps worse, upon a chapter in the life of that little, beautiful brother whom we once all had, and whom we have all lost and mourned, the man we ought to have been, the man we hoped to be. But when word has been passed (even to an editor), it should, if possible, be kept; and if sometimes I am wise and say too little, and sometimes weak and say too much, the blame must lie at the door of the person who entrapped me.

The most influential books,[3] and the truest in their influence, are works of fiction. They do not pin the reader to a dogma, which he must afterwards discover to be inexact; they do not teach him a lesson, which he must afterwards unlearn. They repeat, they rearrange, they clarify the lessons of life; they disengage us from ourselves, they constrain us to the acquaintance of others; and they show us the web of experience, not as we can see it for ourselves, but with a singular change—that monstrous, consuming *ego* of ours being, for the nonce, struck out. To be so, they must be reasonably true to the human comedy; and any work that is so serves the turn of instruction. But the course of our education is answered best by those poems and romances where we breathe a magnanimous atmosphere of thought and meet generous and pious characters. Shakespeare has served me best. Few living friends have had upon me an influence so strong for good as Hamlet or Rosalind. The last character, already well beloved in the reading, I had the good fortune to see, I must think, in an impressionable hour, played by Mrs. Scott Siddons.[4] Nothing has ever more moved, more delighted, more refreshed me; nor has the influence quite passed away. Kent's brief speech[5] over the dying Lear had a great effect upon my mind, and was the burthen of my reflections for long, so profoundly, so touchingly generous did it appear in sense, so overpowering in expression. Perhaps my dearest and best friend outside of Shakespeare is D'Artagnan—the elderly D'Artagnan of the *Vicomte de Bragelonne*.[6] I know not a more human soul, nor, in his way, a finer; I shall be very sorry for the man who is so much of a pedant in morals that he cannot learn from the Captain of Musketeers. Lastly, I must name the *Pilgrim's Progress*,[7] a book that breathes of every beautiful and valuable emotion.

But of works of art little can be said; their influence is profound and silent, like the influence of nature; they mould by contact; we drink them up like water, and are bettered, yet know not how. It is in books more specifically didactic that we can follow out the effect, and distinguish and weigh and compare. A book which has been very influential upon me fell early into my hands, and so may stand first, though I think its influence was only sensible later on, and perhaps still keeps growing, for it is a book not easily outlived: the *Essais* of Montaigne.[8] That temperate and genial picture of life is a great gift to place in the hands of persons of to-day; they will find in these smiling pages a magazine of heroism and wisdom, all of an antique strain; they will have their "linen decencies"[9] and excited orthodoxies fluttered, and will (if they have any gift of reading) perceive that these have not been fluttered without some excuse and ground of reason; and (again if they have any gift of reading) they will end by seeing that this old gentleman was in a dozen ways a finer fellow, and held in a dozen ways a nobler view of life, than they or their contemporaries.

The next book, in order of time, to influence me, was the New Testament, and in particular the Gospel according to St. Matthew. I believe it would startle and move any one if they could make a certain effort of imagination and read it freshly like a book, not droningly and dully like a portion of the Bible. Any one would then be able to see in it those truths which we are all courteously supposed to know and all modestly refrain from applying. But upon this subject it is perhaps better to be silent.

I come next to Whitman's *Leaves of Grass*,[10] a book of singular service, a book which tumbled the world upside down for me, blew into space a thousand cobwebs of genteel and ethical illusion, and, having thus shaken my tabernacle of lies, set me back again upon a strong foundation of all the original and manly virtues. But it is, once more, only a book for those who have the gift of reading.[11] I will be very frank—I believe it is so with all good books except, perhaps, fiction. The average man lives, and must live, so wholly in convention, that gun-powder charges of the truth are more apt to discompose than to invigorate his creed. Either he cries out upon blasphemy and indecency, and crouches the closer round that little idol of part-truths and part-conveniences which is the contemporary deity, or he is convinced by what is new, forgets what is old, and becomes truly blasphemous and indecent himself. New truth is only useful to supplement the old; rough truth is only wanted to expand, not to destroy, our civil and often elegant conventions. He who cannot judge had better stick to fiction and the daily papers. There he will get little harm, and, in the first at least, some good.

Close upon the back of my discovery of Whitman, I came under the influence of Herbert Spencer.[12] No more persuasive rabbi exists. How much of his vast structure will bear the touch of time, how much is clay and how much brass, it were too curious to inquire. But his words, if dry, are always manly and honest; there dwells in his pages a spirit of highly abstract joy, plucked naked like an algebraic symbol but still joyful; and the reader will find there a *caput mortuum*[13] of piety, with little indeed of its loveliness, but with most of its essentials; and these two qualities make him a wholesome, as his intellectual vigour makes him a bracing, writer. I should be much of a hound if I lost my gratitude to Herbert Spencer.

Goethe's Life, by Lewes,[14] had a great importance for me when it first fell into my hands—a strange instance of the partiality of man's good and man's evil. I know no one whom I less admire than Goethe; he seems a very epitome of the sins of genius, breaking open the doors of private life, and wantonly wounding friends, in that crowning offence of *Werther*, and in his own character a mere pen-and-ink Napoleon, conscious of the rights and duties of superior talents as a Spanish inquisitor was conscious of the rights and duties of his office. And yet in his fine devotion to his art, in his honest and serviceable friendship for Schiller, what lessons are contained! Biography, usually so false to its office, does here for once perform for us some of the work of fiction, reminding us, that is, of the truly mingled tissue of man's nature, and how huge faults and shining virtues cohabit and persevere in the same character. History serves us well to this effect, but in the originals, not in the pages of the popular epitomiser, who is bound, by the very nature of his task, to make us feel the difference of epochs instead of the essential identity of man, and even in the originals only to those who can recognise their own human virtues and defects in strange forms, often inverted and under strange names, often interchanged. Martial[15] is a poet of no good repute, and it gives a man new thoughts to read his works dispassionately, and find in this unseemly jester's serious passages the image of a kind, wise, and self-respecting gentleman. It is customary, I suppose, in reading Martial, to leave out these pleasant verses; I never heard of them, at least, until I found them for myself; and this partiality is one among a thousand things that help to build up our distorted and hysterical conception of the great Roman Empire.

This brings us by a natural transition to a very noble book—the *Meditations* of Marcus Aurelius.[16] The dispassionate gravity, the noble forgetfulness of self, the tenderness of others, that are there expressed and were practised on so great a scale in the life of its writer, make this book a book quite by itself. No one can read it and not be moved. Yet it scarcely or rarely appeals to the feelings—those very mobile, those not very trusty parts of man. Its address lies further back: its lesson comes more deeply home; when you have read, you carry away with you a memory of the man himself; it is as though you had touched a loyal hand, looked into brave eyes, and made a noble friend; there is another bond on you thenceforward, binding you to life and to the love of virtue.

Wordsworth[17] should perhaps come next. Every one has been influenced by Wordsworth, and it is hard to tell precisely how. A certain innocence, a rugged austerity of joy, a night of the stars, "the silence that is in the lonely hills," something of the cold thrill of dawn, cling to his work and give it a particular address to what is best in us. I do not know that you learn a lesson; you need not—Mill did not—agree with any one of his beliefs; and yet the spell is cast. Such are the best teachers: a dogma learned is only a new error—the old one was perhaps as good; but a spirit communicated is a perpetual possession. These best teachers climb beyond teaching to the plane of art; it is themselves, and what is best in themselves, that they communicate.

I should never forgive myself if I forgot *The Egoist*. It is art, if you like, but it belongs purely to didactic art, and from all the novels I have read (and I have read thousands) stands in a place by itself. Here is a Nathan for the modern David;[18] here is a book to send the blood into men's faces. Satire, the angry picture of human faults, is not great art; we can all be angry with our neighbour; what we want is to be shown, not his defects, of which we are too conscious, but his merits, to which we are too blind. And *The Egoist*[19] is a satire; so much must be allowed; but it is a satire of a singular quality, which tells you nothing of that obvious mote, which is engaged from first to last with that invisible beam. It is yourself that is hunted down; these are your own faults that are dragged into the day and numbered, with lingering relish, with cruel cunning and precision. A young friend of Mr. Meredith's (as I have the story) came to him in an agony. "This is too bad of you," he cried. "Willoughby is me!" "No, my dear fellow," said the author; "he is all of us." I have read *The Egoist* five or six times myself, and I mean to read it again; for I am like the young friend of the anecdote—I think Willoughby an unmanly but a very serviceable exposure of myself.

I suppose, when I am done, I shall find that I have forgotten much that was most influential, as I see already I have forgotten Thoreau,[20] and Hazlitt, whose paper "On the Spirit of Obligations" was a turning-point in my life, and Penn, whose little book of aphorisms had a brief but strong effect on me, and Mitford's *Tales[21] of Old Japan*, wherein I learned for the first time the proper attitude of any rational man to his country's laws—a secret found, and kept, in the Asiatic islands. That I should commemorate all is more than I can hope or the Editor could ask. It will be more to the point, after having said so much upon improving books, to say a word or two about the improvable reader. The gift of reading, as I have called it, is not very common, nor very generally understood. It consists, first of all, in a vast intellectual endowment—a free grace, I find I must call it— by which a man rises to understand that he is not punctually right, nor those from whom he differs absolutely wrong. He may hold dogmas; he may hold them passionately; and he may know that others hold them but coldly, or hold them differently, or hold them not at all. Well, if he has the gift of reading, these others will be full of meat for him. They will see the other side of propositions and the other side of virtues. He need not change his dogma for that, but he may change his reading of that dogma, and he must supplement and correct his deductions from it. A human truth, which is always very much a lie, hides as much of life as it displays. It is men who hold another truth, or, as it seems to us, perhaps, a dangerous lie, who can extend our restricted field of knowledge, and rouse our drowsy consciences. Something that seems quite new, or that seems insolently false or very dangerous, is the test of a reader. If he tries to see what it means, what truth excuses it, he has the gift, and let him read. If he is merely hurt, or offended, or exclaims upon his author's folly, he had better take to the daily papers; he will never be a reader.

And here, with the aptest illustrative force, after I have laid down my part-truth, I must step in with its opposite. For, after all, we are vessels of a very limited content. Not all men can read all books; it is only in a chosen few that any man will find his appointed food; and the fittest lessons are the most palatable, and make themselves welcome to the mind. A writer learns this early, and it is his chief support; he goes on unafraid, laying down the law; and he is sure at heart that most of what he says is demonstrably false, and much of a mingled strain, and some hurtful, and very little good for service; but he is sure besides that when his words fall into the hands of any genuine reader, they will be weighed and winnowed, and only that which suits will be assimilated; and when they fall into the hands of one who cannot intelligently read, they come there quite silent and inarticulate, falling upon deaf ears, and his secret is kept as if he had not written.

NOTES

This article first appeared in the *British Weekly* for 13 May 1887, forming Stevenson's contribution to a symposium on this subject by some of the celebrated writers of the day, including Gladstone, Ruskin, Hamerton; and others as widely different as Archdeacon Farrar and Rider Haggard. In the same year (1887) the papers were all collected and published by the *Weekly* in a volume, with the title *Books Which Have Influenced Me*. This essay was later included in the complete editions of Stevenson's *Works* (Edinburgh ed., Vol. XI, Thistle ed., Vol. XXII).

[Note 1: First published in the *British Weekly*, May 13, 1887.]

[Note 2: Of the *British Weekly*.]

[Note 3: *The most influential books ... are works of fiction*. This statement is undoubtedly true, if we use the word "fiction" in the sense understood here by Stevenson. It is curious, however, to note the rise in dignity of "works of fiction," and of "novels"; people used to read them with apologies, and did not like to be caught at it. The cheerful audacity of Stevenson's declaration would have seemed like blasphemy fifty years earlier.]

[Note 4: *Mrs. Scott Siddons*. Not for a moment to be confounded with the great actress Sarah Siddons, who died in 1831. Mrs. Scott Siddons, in spite of Stevenson's enthusiasm, was not an actress of remarkable power.]

[Note 5: *Kent's brief speech*. Toward the end of *King Lear*.]

"Vex not his ghost: O, let him pass! he hates him
That would upon the rack of this tough world
Stretch him out longer."]

[Note 6: *D'Artagnan ... Vicomte de Bragelonne*. See Stevenson's essay, *A Gossip on a Novel of Dumas's* (1887), in *Memories and Portraits*. See also Note 3 of Chapter II above and Note 43 of Chapter IV above. *Vicomte de Bragelonne* is the title of the sequel to *Twenty Years After*, which is the sequel to the *Musketeers*. Dumas wrote 257 volumes of romance, plays, travels etc.]

[Note 7: *Pilgrim's Progress*. See Note 13 of Chapter V above.]

[Note 8: *Essais of Montaigne*. See Note 6 of Chapter VI above. The best translation in English of the *Essais* is that by the Elizabethan, John Florio (1550-1625), a contemporary of Montaigne. His translation appeared in 1603, and may now be obtained complete in the handy "Temple" classics. There is a copy of Florio's *Montaigne* with Ben Jonson's autograph, and also one that has what many believe to be a genuine autograph of Shakspere.]

[Note 9: "*Linen decencies.*" "The ghost of a linen decency yet haunts us."—Milton, *Areopagitica.*]

[Note 10: *Whitman's Leaves of Grass.* See Stevenson's admirable essay on *Walt Whitman* (1878), also Note 12 of Chapter III above.]

[Note 11: *Have the gift of reading.* "Books are written to be read by those who can understand them. Their possible effect on those who cannot, is a matter of medical rather than of literary interest." —Prof. W. Raleigh, *The English Novel,* remarks on *Tom Jones,* Chap. VI.]

[Note 12: *Herbert.* See Note 18 of Chapter IV above.]

[Note 13: *Caput mortuum.* Dry kernel. Literary, "dead head."]

[Note 14: *Goethe's Life, by Lewes.* The standard Life of Goethe (in English) is still that by George Henry Lewes (1817-1878), the husband of George Eliot. His *Life of Goethe* appeared in 1855; he later made a simpler, abridged edition, called *The Story of Goethe's Life.* Goethe, the greatest literary genius since Shakspere, and now generally ranked among the four supreme writers of the world, Homer, Dante, Shakspere, Goethe, was born in 1749, and died in 1832. Stevenson, like most British critics, is rather severe on Goethe's character. The student should read Eckermann's *Conversations with Goethe*, a book full of wisdom and perennial delight. For *Werther*, see Note 18 of Chapter VI above. The friendship between Goethe and Schiller (1759-1805), "his honest and serviceable friendship," as Stevenson puts it, is among the most beautiful things to contemplate in literary history. Before the theatre in Weimar, Germany, where the two men lived, stands a remarkable statue of the pair: and their coffins lie side by side in a crypt in the same town.]

[Note 15: *Martial.* Poet, wit and epigrammatist, born in Spain 43 A. D., died 104. He lived in Rome from 66 to 100, enjoying a high reputation as a writer.]

[Note 16: *Meditations of Marcus Aurelius.* Marcus Aurelius Antoninus, often called "the noblest of Pagans" was born 121 A. D., and died 180. His *Meditations* have been translated into the chief modern languages, and though their author was hostile to Christianity, the ethics of the book are much the same as those of the New Testament.]

[Note 17: *Wordsworth … Mill.* William Wordsworth (1770-1850), poet-laureate (1843-1850), is by many regarded as the third poet in English literature, after Shakspere and Milton, whose places are unassailable. Other candidates for the third place are Chaucer and Spenser. "The silence that is in the lonely hills" is loosely quoted from Wordsworth's *Song at the Feast of Brougham Castle, Upon the Restoration of Lord Clifford*, published in 1807. The passage reads:

"The silence that is in the starry sky,

The sleep that is among the lonely hills."

... In the *Autobiography* (1873) of John Stuart Mill (1806-1873), there is a remarkable passage where he testifies to the influence exerted upon him by Wordsworth.]

[Note 18: *A Nathan for the modern David.* The famous accusation of the prophet to the king, "Thou art the man." See II *Sam.* 12.]

[Note 19: *The Egoist.* See Note 47 of Chapter IV above. Stevenson never tired of singing the praises of this novel.]

[Note 20: *Thoreau ... Hazlitt ... Penn ... Mitford's Tales...* Henry David Thoreau (1817-1862), the American naturalist and writer, whose works impressed Stevenson deeply. See the latter's excellent essay on Thoreau (1880), in *Familiar Studies of Men and Books....* Hazlitt, See Note 19 of Chapter II above. His paper, *On the Spirit of Obligations*, appeared in *The Plain Speaker*, 2 Vols., 1826. *Penn, whose little book of aphorisms.* This refers to William Penn's famous book, *Some Fruits of Solitude: in Reflections and Maxims relating to the Conduct of Human Life* (1693). Edmund Gosse says, in his Introduction to a charming little edition of this book in 1900, "Stevenson had intended to make this book and its author the subject of one of his critical essays. In February 1880 he was preparing to begin it... He never found the opportunity... But it has left an indelible stamp on the tenor of his moral writings. The philosophy of B. L. S. ... is tinctured through and through with the honest, shrewd, and genial maxims of Penn." Stevenson himself, in his *Letters* (Vol. I, pp. 232, 233), spoke of this little book in the highest terms of praise.]

[Note 21: *Mitford's Tales.* Mary Russell Mitford (1787-1855), a novelist and dramatist who enjoyed an immense vogue. "Her inimitable series of country sketches, drawn from her own experiences at Three Mile Cross, entitled 'Our Village,' began to appear in 1819 in the 'Lady's Magazine,' a little-known periodical, whose sale was thereby increased from 250 to 2,000. ... The sketches had an enormous success, and were collected in five volumes, published respectively in 1824, 1826, 1828, 1830, and 1832. ... The book may be said to have laid the foundation of a branch of literature hitherto untried. The sketches resemble Dutch paintings in their fidelity of detail."—*Dic. Nat. Biog.*]

IX

PULVIS ET UMBRA

We look for some reward of our endeavors and are disappointed; not success, not happiness, not even peace of conscience, crowns our ineffectual efforts to do well. Our frailties are invincible, are virtues barren; the battle goes sore against us to the going down of the sun. The canting moralist tells us of right and wrong; and we look abroad, even on the face of our small earth, and find them change with every climate,[1] and no country where some action is not honoured for a virtue and none where it is not branded for a vice; and we look in our experience, and find no vital congruity in the wisest rules, but at the best a municipal fitness. It is not strange if we are tempted to despair of good. We ask too much. Our religions and moralities have been trimmed to flatter us, till they are all emasculate and sentimentalised, and only please and weaken. Truth is of a rougher strain. In the harsh face of life, faith can read a bracing gospel. The human race is a thing more ancient than the ten commandments; and the bones and revolutions of the Kosmos, in whose joints we are but moss and fungus, more ancient still.

I

Of the Kosmos in the last resort, science reports many doubtful things and all of them appalling. There seems no substance to this solid globe on which we stamp: nothing but symbols and ratios. Symbols and ratios carry us and bring us forth and beat us down; gravity that swings the incommensurable suns and worlds through space, is but a figment varying inversely as the squares of distances; and the suns and worlds themselves, imponderable figures of abstraction, NH3 and H2O.[2] Consideration dares not dwell upon this view; that way madness lies;[3] science carries us into zones of speculation, where there is no habitable city for the mind of man.

But take the Kosmos with a grosser faith, as our senses give it to us. We behold space sown with rotatory islands; suns and worlds and the shards and wrecks of systems: some, like the sun, still blazing; some rotting, like the earth; others, like the moon, stable in desolation. All of these we take to be made of something we call matter: a thing which no analysis can help us to conceive; to whose incredible properties no familiarity can reconcile our minds. This stuff, when not purified by the lustration of fire, rots uncleanly into something we call life; seized through all its atoms with a pediculous malady; swelling in tumours that become independent, sometimes even (by an abhorrent prodigy) locomotory;[4] one splitting into millions, millions cohering

210

into one, as the malady proceeds through varying stages. This vital putrescence of the dust, used as we are to it, yet strikes us with occasional disgust, and the profusion of worms in a piece of ancient turf, or the air of a marsh darkened with insects, will sometimes check our breathing so that we aspire for cleaner places. But none is clean: the moving sand is infected with lice; the pure spring, where it bursts out of the mountain, is a mere issue of worms; even in the hard rock the crystal is forming.

In two main shapes this eruption covers the countenance of the earth: the animal and the vegetable: one in some degree the inversion of the other: the second rooted to the spot; the first coming detached out of its natal mud, and scurrying abroad with the myriad feet of insects or towering into the heavens on the wings of birds: a thing so inconceivable that, if it be well considered, the heart stops. To what passes with the anchored vermin, we have little clue: doubtless they have their joys and sorrows, their delights and killing agonies: it appears not how. But of the locomotory, to which we ourselves belong, we can tell more. These share with us a thousand miracles: the miracles of sight, of hearing, of the projection of sound, things that bridge space; the miracles of memory and reason, by which the present is conceived, and when it is gone, its image kept living in the brains of man and brute; the miracle of reproduction, with its imperious desires and staggering consequences. And to put the last touch upon this mountain mass of the revolting and the inconceivable, all these prey upon each other, lives tearing other lives in pieces, cramming them inside themselves, and by that summary process, growing fat: the vegetarian, the whale, perhaps the tree, not less than the lion of the desert; for the vegetarian is only the eater of the dumb.

Meanwhile our rotary island loaded with predatory life, and more drenched with blood, both animal and vegetable, than ever mutinied ship, scuds through space with unimaginable speed, and turns alternate cheeks to the reverberation of a blazing world, ninety million miles away.

II

What a monstrous spectre is this man, the disease of the agglutinated dust, lifting alternate feet or lying drugged with slumber; killing, feeding, growing, bringing forth small copies of himself; grown upon with hair like grass, fitted with eyes that move and glitter in his face; a thing to set children screaming;—and yet looked at nearlier, known as his fellows know him, how surprising are his attributes! Poor soul, here for so little, cast among so many hardships, filled with desires so incommensurate and so inconsistent, savagely surrounded, savagely descended, irremediably condemned to prey upon his fellow lives: who should have blamed him had he been of a piece with his destiny and a being merely barbarous? And we look and behold him instead filled with imperfect virtues: infinitely childish, often admirably valiant, often touchingly kind; sitting down, amidst his momentary life, to debate of right and wrong and the attributes of the deity; rising up to do battle for an egg or die for an idea; singling out his friends and his mate with cordial affection; bringing forth in pain, rearing with long-suffering solicitude, his young. To touch the heart of his mystery,[5] we find in him one thought, strange to the point of lunacy: the thought of duty;[6] the thought of something owing to himself, to his neighbour, to his God: an ideal of decency, to which he would rise if it were possible; a limit of shame, below which, if it be possible, he will not stoop. The design in most men is one of conformity; here and there, in picked natures, it transcends itself and soars on the other side, arming martyrs with independence; but in all, in their degrees, it is a bosom thought:—Not in man alone, for we trace it in dogs and cats whom we know fairly well, and doubtless some similar point of honour sways the elephant, the oyster, and the louse, of whom we know so little:—But in man, at least, it sways with so complete an empire that merely selfish things come second, even with the selfish: that appetites are starved, fears are conquered, pains supported; that almost the dullest shrinks from the reproof of a glance, although it were a child's; and all but the most cowardly stand amid the risks of war; and the more noble, having strongly conceived an act as due to their ideal, affront and embrace death. Strange enough if, with their singular origin and perverted practice, they think they are to be rewarded in some future life: stranger still, if they are persuaded of the contrary, and think this blow, which they solicit, will strike them senseless for eternity. I shall be reminded what a tragedy of misconception and misconduct man at large presents: of organised injustice, cowardly violence and treacherous crime; and of the damning imperfections of the best. They cannot be too darkly drawn. Man is indeed marked for failure in his efforts to do right. But where the best consistently miscarry, how tenfold more remarkable that all should continue to strive; and surely we should find it both touching and inspiriting, that in a field from which success is banished, our race should not cease to labour.

If the first view of this creature, stalking in his rotatory isle, be a thing to shake the courage of the stoutest, on this nearer sight, he startles us with an admiring wonder. It matters not where we look, under what climate we observe him, in what stage of society, in what depth of ignorance, burthened with what erroneous morality; by camp-fires in Assiniboia,[7] the snow powdering his shoulders, the wind plucking his blanket, as he sits, passing the ceremonial calumet and uttering his grave opinions like a Roman senator; in ships at sea, a man inured to hardship and vile pleasures, his brightest hope a fiddle in a tavern and a bedizened trull who sells herself to rob him, and he for all that simple, innocent, cheerful, kindly like a child, constant to toil, brave to drown, for others; in the slums of cities, moving among indifferent millions to mechanical employments, without hope of change in the future, with scarce a pleasure in the present, and yet true to his virtues, honest up to his lights, kind to his neighbours, tempted perhaps in vain by the bright gin-palace, perhaps long-suffering with the drunken wife that ruins him; in India (a woman this time) kneeling with broken cries and streaming tears, as she drowns her child in the sacred river;[8] in the brothel, the discard of society, living mainly on strong drink, fed with affronts, a fool, a thief, the comrade of thieves, and even here keeping the point of honour and the touch of pity,[9] often repaying the world's scorn with service, often standing firm upon a scruple, and at a certain cost, rejecting riches:—everywhere some virtue cherished or affected, everywhere some decency of thought and carriage, everywhere the ensign of man's ineffectual goodness:—ah! if I could show you this! if I could show you these men and women, all the world over, in every stage of history, under every abuse of error, under every circumstance of failure, without hope, without help, without thanks, still obscurely fighting the lost fight of virtue, still clinging, in the brothel or on the scaffold, to some rag of honour, the poor jewel of their souls! They may seek to escape, and yet they cannot; it is not alone their privilege and glory, but their doom; they are condemned to some nobility; all their lives long, the desire of good is at their heels, the implacable hunter.

Of all earth's meteors, here at least is the most strange and consoling: that this ennobled lemur, this hair-crowned bubble of the dust, this inheritor of a few years and sorrows, should yet deny himself his rare delights, and add to his frequent pains, and live for an ideal, however misconceived. Nor can we stop with man. A new doctrine,[10] received with screams a little while ago by canting moralists, and still not properly worked into the body of our thoughts, lights us a step farther into the heart of this rough but noble universe. For nowadays the pride of man denies in vain his kinship with the original dust. He stands no longer like a thing apart. Close at his heels we see the dog, prince of another genius: and in him too, we see dumbly testified the same cultus[11] of an unattainable ideal, the same constancy in failure. Does it stop with the dog? We look at our feet where the ground is blackened with the swarming ant: a creature so small, so far from us in the hierarchy of brutes, that we can scarce trace and scarce comprehend his doings; and here also, in his ordered polities and rigorous justice, we see confessed the law of duty and the fact of individual sin. Does it stop, then, with the ant? Rather this desire of well-doing and this doom of frailty run through all the grades of life: rather is this earth, from the frosty top of Everest[12] to the next margin of the internal fire, one stage of ineffectual virtues and one temple of pious tears and perseverance. The whole creation groaneth[13] and travaileth together. It is the common and the god-like law of life. The browsers, the biters, the barkers, the hairy coats of field and forest, the squirrel in the oak, the thousand-footed creeper in the dust, as they share with us the gift of life, share with us the love of an ideal: strive like us—like us are tempted to grow weary of the struggle—to do well; like us receive at times unmerited refreshment, visitings of support, returns of courage; and are condemned like us to be crucified between that double law[14] of the members and the will. Are they like us, I wonder in the timid hope of some reward, some sugar with the drug? do they, too, stand aghast at unrewarded virtues, at the sufferings of those whom, in our partiality, we take to be just, and the prosperity of such as, in our blindness, we call wicked? It may be, and yet God knows what they should look for. Even while they look, even while they repent, the foot of man treads them by thousands in the dust, the yelping hounds burst upon their trail, the bullet speeds, the knives are heating in the den of the vivisectionist;[15] or the dew falls, and the generation of a day is blotted out. For these are creatures, compared with whom our weakness is strength, our ignorance wisdom, our brief span eternity.

And as we dwell, we living things, in our isle of terror[16] and under the imminent hand of death, God forbid it should be man the erected, the reasoner, the wise in his own eyes—God forbid it should be man that wearies in well-doing,[17] that despairs of unrewarded effort, or utters the language of complaint. Let it be enough for faith, that the whole creation groans in mortal frailty, strives with unconquerable constancy: Surely not all in vain.[18]

NOTES

During the year 1888, part of which was spent by Stevenson at Saranac Lake in the Adirondacks he published one article every month in *Scribner's Magazine*. *Pulvis et Umbra* appeared in the April number, and was later included in the volume *Across the Plains* (1892). He wrote this particular essay with intense feeling. Writing to Sidney Colvin in December 1887, he said, "I get along with my papers for *Scribner* not fast, nor so far specially well; only this last, the fourth one.... I do believe is pulled off after a fashion. It is a mere sermon: ... but it is true, and I find it touching and beneficial, to me at least; and I think there is some fine writing in it, some very apt and pregnant phrases. *Pulvis et Umbra*, I call it; I might have called it a *Darwinian Sermon*, if I had wanted. Its sentiments, although parsonic, will not offend even you, I believe." (*Letters*, II, 100.) Writing to Miss Adelaide Boodle in April 1888, he said, "I wrote a paper the other day—*Pulvis et Umbra*;—I wrote it with great feeling and conviction: to me it seemed bracing and healthful, it is in such a world (so seen by me), that I am very glad to fight out my battle, and see some fine sunsets, and hear some

excellent jests between whiles round the camp fire. But I find that
to some people this vision of mine is a nightmare, and extinguishes
all ground of faith in God or pleasure in man. Truth I think not
so much of; for I do not know it. And I could wish in my heart
that I had not published this paper, if it troubles folk too much: all
have not the same digestion nor the same sight of things…. Well,
I cannot take back what I have said; but yet I may add this. If my
view be everything but the nonsense that it may be—to me it seems
self-evident and blinding truth—surely of all things it makes this
world holier. There is nothing in it but the moral side—but the
great battle and the breathing times with their refreshments. I see
no more and no less. And if you look again, it is not ugly, and it is
filled with promise." (*Letters*, II, 123.) The words *Pulvis et Umbra*
mean literally "dust and shadow": the phrase, however, is quoted
from Horace "pulvis et umbra sumus"—*we are dust and ashes*. It
forms the text of one of Stevenson's familiar discourses on Death,
like *Aes Triplex*.

[Note 1: *Find them change with every climate*, etc. For some
striking illustrations of this, see Sudermann's drama, *Die Ehre*
(Honour).]

[Note 2: NH3 and H2O. The first is the chemical formula
for ammonia: the second, for water.]

[Note 3: *That way madness lies. King Lear*, III, 4, 21.]

[Note 4: *A pediculous malady … locomotory*. Stevenson was
fond of strange words. "Pediculous" means covered with lice, lousy.]

[Note 5: *The heart of his mystery.* Hamlet, Act III, Sc. 2, "you would pluck out the heart of my mystery." Mystery here means "secret," as in I. *Cor.* XIII, "Behold, I tell you a mystery."]

[Note 6: *The thought of duty.* Kant said, "Two things fill the mind with ever new and increasing admiration and awe, the oftener and the more steadily we reflect on them: *the starry heavens above and the moral law within.*" (Conclusion to the *Practical Reason—Kritik der praktischen Vernunft*, 1788.)]

[Note 7: *Assiniboia … Calumet.* Assinibioia is a district of Canada, just west of Manitoba. *Calumet* is the pipe of peace, used by
North American Indians when solemnizing treaties etc. Its stem is over
two feet long, heavily decorated with feathers etc.]

[Note 8: *Drowns her child in the sacred river.* The sacred river of India is the Ganges; before British control, children were often sacrificed there by drowning to appease the angry divinity.]

[Note 9: *The touch of pity.* "No beast so fierce but knows some touch of pity." *Richard III*, Act I, Sc. 2, vs. 71. *This ennobled lemur.* A lemur is a nocturnal animal, something like a monkey.]

[Note 10: *A new doctrine.* Evolution. Darwin's *Origin of Species* was published in 1859. Many ardent Christians believe in its general principles to-day; but at first it was bitterly attacked by orthodox and conservative critics. A Princeton professor cried, "Darwinism is Atheism!"]

[Note 11: *Cultus.* Stevenson liked this word. *The swarming ant.* "The ants are a people not strong, yet they prepare their meat in the summer."—*Proverbs*, XXX. 25. For a wonderful description of an ant battle, see Thoreau's *Walden.*]

[Note 12: *Everest.* Mount Everest in the Himalayas, is the highest mountain in the world, with an altitude of about 29,000 feet.]

[Note 13: *The whole creation groaneth. Romans*, VIII, 22.]

[Note 14: *That double law of the members.* See Note 10 of Chapter VI above.]

[Note 15: *Den of the vivisectionist.* See Note 2 of Chapter VI above.]

[Note 16: *In our isle of terror.* Cf. Herriet, *The White Island.*

"In this world, the isle of dreams,

While we sit by sorrow's streams,

Tears and terrors are our themes."]

[Note 17: *Man that wearies in well-doing. Galatians*, VI, 9.]

[Note 18: *Surely not all in vain.* At heart, Stevenson belongs not to the pessimists nor the skeptics, but to the optimists and the believers. A man may have no formal creed, and yet be a believer.